Edvina

DDC

Quick Reference Guide

WordPerfect 5.1™

IBM PC

SALAZAR / CASSANO / SCHWARTZ

DDC
Dictation Disc Company

INTRODUCTION

Quick Reference Guide for WordPerfect 5.1™ will assist you in working with WordPerfect 5.1 software.

This handy guide will save you hours of searching through technical manuals. Each step is illustrated so that at a quick glance you will be able to execute even the most complicated WordPerfect functions.

WordPerfect allows you to select menu options in a variety of ways:

Selecting the <u>number</u> of the option (1, 2, 3, etc).
Typing the <u>letter</u> that is in reverse video in each item.
<u>Highlighting</u> the menu option and pressing ENTER.
Using the mouse to select any of the options above.

We have chosen to illustrate the steps by selecting the letter displayed in reverse video.

A template for the function keys is illustrated on the outside back cover.

It is our hope that this guide will help you use WordPerfect 5.1™ with ease.

Authors
Marivel Salazar
Angelo Cassano
Karl Schwartz

Technical Editor
Paul Berube

Designed and typeset using WordPerfect 5.1 by
Karl Schwartz.

2
STARTUP PROCEDURE/LOADING

FOR TWO FLOPPY DISK DRIVES

NOTE: To run WordPerfect 5.1 on a two floppy disk system each drive must be 720k or larger.

1. Insert DOS disk into drive A.
2. Turn computer on.
3. Type Date (**MM-DD-YY**).
4. **Enter**
5. Type Time (**HH:MM:SS**).
6. **Enter**
7. Insert WordPerfect 1 disk into drive A.
8. Insert data disk into drive B.
9. Type **B:**
10. **Enter**
11. Type **A:wp**
12. **Enter**
13. Replace Wordperfect 1 disk with WordPerfect 2 disk.
14. **Enter**

NOTE: Steps 13-14 are not required for 3.5 disks.

FOR HARD DISK DRIVE WITH FLOPPY DISK

1. Turn computer on.

NOTE: DOS must be in directory path.

2. Insert Data Disk into drive A.
3. Change to WordPerfect directory.
4. Type **WP**
5. **Enter**
6. **Enter**

CREATE A DOCUMENT

NOTE: *After starting WordPerfect, the cursor will blink in the top left-hand corner of the screen. The status line appears at the bottom right-hand corner of the screen, and displays the document number, page number, line and cursor position. The line and position are measured in inches.*

Begin typing text.

Example: Doc 1 Pg 1 Ln 1" Pos 1"

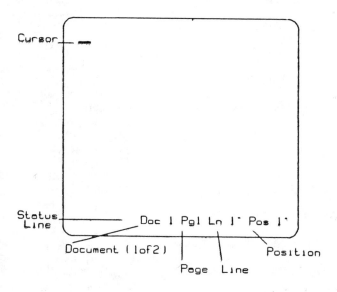

4
CURSOR MOVEMENTS WITHIN A DOCUMENT

One character left . . . . `←`

One character right . . . . `→`

One line up . . . . `↑`

One line down . . . . `↓`

Previous word . . . . `Ctrl`+`←`

Next word . . . . `Ctrl`+`→`

Top of previous page . . . . `PgUp`

Top of next page . . . . `PgDn`

Top of screen . . . . `Home` `↑`

End of screen . . . . `Home` `↓`

Left of screen . . . . `Home` `←`

Right of screen . . . . `Home` `→`

Beginning of document . . . . . . `Home` `Home` `↑`

End of document . . . . `Home` `Home` `↓`

Beginning of Line . . . . `Home` `Home` `←`

End of Line . . . . `Home` `Home` `→`

One paragraph up . . . . `Ctrl`+`↑`

One paragraph down . . . . `Ctrl`+`↓`

Top of page . . . . `Ctrl`+`Home` `↑`

Bottom of Page . . . . `Ctrl`+`Home` `↓`

5

CURSOR MOVEMENTS USING GO TO

TO A SPECIFIC CHARACTER
1. Press **Ctrl + Home** (Go To) . . . . . . `Ctrl`+`Home`
2. Type character . . . . Character

TO A SPECIFIC PAGE
1. Press **Ctrl + Home** (Go To) . . . . . . `Ctrl`+`Home`
2. Type page number . . . . Number
3. **Enter** . . . . `⏎`

TO TOP OF CURRENT PAGE
1. Press **Ctrl + Home** (Go To) . . . . . . `Ctrl`+`Home`
2. Press **Up Arrow** . . . . `↑`

TO BOTTOM OF CURRENT PAGE
1. Press **Ctrl + Home** (Go To) . . . . . . `Ctrl`+`Home`
2. Press **Down Arrow** . . . . `↓`

6
SAVING A DOCUMENT

SAVE NEW DOCUMENT AND CONTINUE WORKING

1. Press **F10** (Save) . . . . `F10`

OR	Pull-down Menu	OR
A) Press **Alt + =**		`Alt`+`=`
B) Select **F** (File)		`F`
C) Select **S** (Save)		`S`

2. Type document name . . . . Filename

   NOTE: *If necessary, indicate drive/directory when*
   entering document name.
   Example: *A:\DOCS\LETTER*

3. **Enter** . . . . `↵`

SAVE AND EXIT NEW DOCUMENT

1. Press **F7** (Exit) . . . . `F7`

OR	Pull-down Menu	OR
A) Press **Alt + =**		`Alt`+`=`
B) Select **F** (File)		`F`
C) Select **X** (Exit)		`X`

2. **Enter** . . . . `↵`

3. Type document name . . . . Filename

   NOTE: *If necessary, indicate drive/directory when*
   entering document name.
   Example: *A:\DOCS\LETTER*

4. **Enter** . . . . `↵`

5. **Enter** (remain in WordPerfect) . . . . `↵`

Saving a document (continued)

SAVE AND EXIT A PREVIOUSLY SAVED DOCUMENT

1. Press **F7** (Exit) . . . . `F7`

OR	Pull-down Menu	OR
A) Press **Alt + =**		`Alt`+`=`
B) Select **F** (File)		`F`
C) Select **X** (Exit)		`X`

2. **Enter** (save document) . . . . `↵`

3. **Enter** (retain same document name) . . . . `↵`

4. Type **Y** (update document with revisions) . . . . `Y`

5. **Enter** (remain in WordPerfect) . . . . `↵`

SAVE AND CONTINUE WORKING ON A PREVIOUSLY SAVED DOCUMENT

1. Press **F10** (Save) . . . . `F10`

OR	Pull-down Menu	OR
A) Press **Alt + =**		`Alt`+`=`
B) Select **F** (File)		`F`
C) Select **S** (Save)		`S`

2. **Enter** (retain same document name) . . . . `↵`

3. Type **Y** (update document with revisions) . . . . . `Y`

8
CLEAR SCREEN

1. Press **F7** (Exit) . . . . `F7`

OR	Pull-down Menu	OR
A) Press **Alt + =**		`Alt`+`=`
B) Select **F** (File)		`F`
C) Select **X** (Exit)		`X`

2. Type **N** . . . . `N`
3. **Enter** . . . . `↵`

RETRIEVE A DOCUMENT

NOTE: If document is on screen see CLEAR SCREEN above.

1. Press **Shift + F10** (Retrieve) . . . . . . `Shift`+`F10`

OR	Pull-down Menu	OR
A) Press **Alt + =**		`Alt`+`=`
B) Select **F** (File)		`F`
C) Select **R** (Retrieve)		`R`

NOTE: If necessary, indicate drive/directory when entering document name.
Example: A:\DOC\LETTER

2. Type name of document to be retrieved . . Filename
3. **Enter** . . . . `↵`

- OR -

Retrieve a document (continued)

LIST FILES

1. Press F5 (List Files) . . . . `F5`

OR	Pull-down Menu	OR
A) Press Alt + = ...		`Alt`+`=`
B) Select F (File)		`F`
C) Select F (List Files)		`F`

   NOTE: *If necessary, change drive/directory to*
            access files. Example: A:\DOC

2. Enter   . . . . `⏎`

3. Use cursor movement keys to highlight
   desired document.

4. Select R (Retrieve) . . . . `R`

10
BLOCK TEXT (Highlighting)

(for Append, Bold, Case Conversion, Center,
Comment, Delete, Flush Right, Font, Mark Text,
Move, Print, Protect, Replace, Save, Search, Shell,
Sort, Spell, Styles, Switch)

1. Place cursor on first character of text to be blocked
   (highlighted).

2. Press **Alt + F4** (Block) . . . . `Alt` + `F4`

OR	Pull-down Menu	OR
A) Press **Alt + =**		`Alt` + `=`
B) Select **E** (Edit)		`E`
C) Select **B** (Block off)		`B`

> *NOTE: A flashing "Block on" message appears at
>   the bottom left-hand corner of the screen.*

3. Highlight text to be defined:

One character to the right . . . . `→`

One word to the right . . . . `Ctrl` + `→`

End of line . . . . `End`

One line up . . . . `↑`

One line down . . . . `↓`

A sentence . . . . `.`

A paragraph . . . . `↵`

End of screen . . . . `Home` `↓`

End of page . . . . `PgDn`

Continued ...

Block text (continued)

Several pages

     a) Press **Ctrl + Home** (Go To). . ⌨️**Ctrl** + **Home**

     b) Type page number . . . . Number

NOTE: *This highlights up to the beginning of the selected page number.*

     c) **Enter** . . . . ⏎

4. Continue to execute specific function.

EDITING TEXT

INSERTING TEXT

NOTE: *If "Typeover" appears in the lower left hand corner of the screen press Insert.*

1. Place cursor where text is to be inserted.

2. Type text.

TYPEOVER

Overwriting text.

1. Place cursor where text is to be overwritten.

2. Press **Insert** . . . . **Ins**

NOTE: *"Typeover" message appears at bottom left corner of the screen.*

3. Type text.

4. Press **Insert** (Typeover off) . . . . **Ins**

12

Editing (continued)

DELETE

Character
1. Place cursor on character to be deleted.
2. Press **Delete** .... `Del`

Previous Character
1. Place cursor one position to right of character to be deleted.
2. Press **Backspace** .... `BkSp`

Word
1. Place cursor on any character of word to be deleted.
2. Press **Ctrl + Backspace** .... `Ctrl`+`BkSp`

Part of Word
From left of cursor to beginning of word.
• Press **Home, Backspace** .... `Home` `BkSp`

From cursor to next word.
• Press **Home, Delete** .... `Home` `Del`

To End of Line
1. Place cursor on first character to be deleted.
2. Press **Ctrl + End** .... `Ctrl`+`End`

Continued ...

Editing (continued)
Delete (continued)

To End of Page
1. Place cursor on first character to be deleted.
2. Press **Ctrl + PgDn** . . . . `Ctrl` + `PgDn`
3. Type **Y** (Delete remainder of page) . . . . `Y`

Several Lines
1. Place cursor on first character to be deleted.
2. Press **Esc** (Repeat) . . . . `Esc`
3. Type number of lines to be deleted . . . . . . Number
4. Press **Ctrl + End** . . . . `Ctrl` + `End`

DELETE USING BLOCK HIGHLIGHT
1. Place cursor on first character to be deleted.
2. Press **Alt + F4** (Block) . . . . `Alt` + `F4`

OR	Pull-down Menu	OR
A) Press **Alt + =**		`Alt` + `=`
B) Select **E** (Edit)		`E`
C) Select **B** (Block)		`B`

3. Highlight text (see Block Text on page 10).
4. Press **Delete** . . . . `Del`
5. Type **Y** (Delete Block) . . . . `Y`

14

DELETE CODES

1. Press **Alt + F3** (Reveal Codes) ...... `Alt`+`F3`

OR	Pull-down Menu	OR
A) Press **Alt + =**		`Alt`+`=`
B) Select **E** (Edit)		`E`
C) Select **R** (Reveal Codes)		`R`

2. Place cursor on code to be deleted.

3. Press **Delete** .... `Del`

4. Press **Alt + F3** (Exit Reveal Codes) ... `Alt`+`F3`

OR	Pull-down Menu	OR
A) Press **Alt + =**		`Alt`+`=`
B) Select **E** (Edit)		`E`
C) Select **R** (Reveal Codes)		`R`

PREVIOUS CODES

1. Press **Alt + F3** (Reveal Codes) ...... `Alt`+`F3`

OR	Pull-down Menu	OR
A) Press **Alt + =**		`Alt`+`=`
B) Select **E** (Edit)		`E`
C) Select **R** (Reveal Codes)		`R`

2. Place cursor one position to right of code to be deleted.

3. Press **Backspace** .... `BkSp`

Continued ...

Editing (continued)
Delete Previous Codes (continued)

4. Press **Alt + F3** (Reveal Codes) ...... `Alt`+`F3`

OR	Pull-down Menu	OR
A) Press **Alt + =**		`Alt`+`=`
B) Select **E** (Edit)		`E`
C) Select **R** (Reveal Codes)		`R`

UNDELETE

1. Place cursor where previously deleted text will be inserted.

2. Press **F1** (Undelete) .... `F1`

OR	Pull-down Menu	OR
A) Press **Alt + =**		`Alt`+`=`
B) Select **E** (Edit)		`E`
C) Select **U** (Undelete)		`U`

3. Select **R** (Restore) .... `R`

   OR   OR

   a) Press **P** (until desired deletion is displayed). . `P`
   NOTE: The last three deletions are stored in memory.
   b) Select **R** (Restore) .... `R`

16
DOCUMENT SUMMARY

CREATE

1. Retrieve document which will contain document summary.

2. Press **Shift + F8** (Format) . . . . **Shift** + **F8**

OR	**Pull-down Menu**	OR
A) Press **Alt + =**		**Alt** + **=**
B) Select **L** (Layout)		**L**

3. Select **D** (Document) . . . . **D**

4. Select **S** (Summary) . . . . **S**

5. Select **D** (Creation **D**ate) . . . . **D**

6. Edit date.

7. **Enter** . . . . **⏎**

8. Select **N** (Document **N**ame/Document Type) . . **N**

   a) Type Long Document Name.

   b) **Enter** . . . . **⏎**

   c) Type category.

   d) **Enter** . . . . **⏎**

9. Select **T** (Author/**T**ypist) . . . . **T**

   a) Type Author.

   b) **Enter** . . . . **⏎**

   c) Type Typist.

   d) **Enter** . . . . **⏎**

Continued ...

Document Summary (continued)
Create (continued) (continued)

10. Select **S** (Subject) . . . . `S`

    a) Type Subject.

    b) **Enter** . . . . `⏎`

11. Select **C** (Account) . . . . `C`

    a) Type Account.

    b) **Enter** . . . . `⏎`

12. Select **K** (Keywords) . . . . `K`

    a) Type keywords.

    b) **Enter** . . . . `⏎`

13. Select **A** (Abstract) . . . . `A`

    a) Type abstract.

    b) **Enter** . . . . `⏎`

14. Press **F7** . . . . `F7`

15. Press **F7** (return to document) . . . . `F7`

18

Document Summary (continued)

EDIT

1. Retrieve document that contains document summary to be edited.

2. Press **Shift + F8** (Format) . . . . `Shift`+`F8`

OR	Pull-down Menu	OR
A) Press **Alt + =**		`Alt`+`=`
B) Select **L** (Layout)		`L`

3. Select **D** (Document) . . . . `D`

4. Select **S** (Summary) . . . . `S`

5. Select **one** of the following: Option

   a) **D** (Creation **D**ate) . . . . `D`

   b) **N** (Document **N**ame) . . . . `N`

   c) **T** (Author/**T**ypist) . . . . `T`

   d) **S** (**S**ubject) . . . . `S`

   e) **C** (A**c**count) . . . . `C`

   f) **K** (**K**eywords) . . . . `K`

   g) **A** (**A**bstract) . . . . `A`

6. Edit text.

7. **Enter** . . . . `↵`

8. Repeat steps 5-7 to edit additional options.

9. Press **F7** . . . . `F7`

10. Press **F7** (return to document) . . . . `F7`

PRINTING

A STORED DOCUMENT

1. Press **Shift + F7** (Print) . . . . **Shift** + **F7**

OR	Pull-down Menu	OR
A) Press **Alt + =**		**Alt** + **=**
B) Select **F** (File)		**F**
C) Select **P** (Print)		**P**

2. Select **D** (Document on disk) . . . . **D**

3. Type document name. . . . . Filename

   NOTE: If necessary, indicate drive/directory
   when entering document name.
   Example: A:\DOCS\LETTER

4. **Enter** . . . .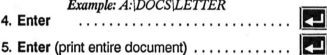

5. **Enter** (print entire document) . . . .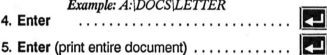

   OR   OR

   a) Type page(s) with commas and dashes.

   Examples:

-3	Pages 1-3
2,5	Pages 2 and 5
4-9	Pages 4-9
6-	Pages 6 to last page
-3, 8-10, 13	Pages 1-3, 8-10, 13

   b) **Enter** . . . .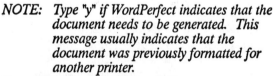

   NOTE: Type "y" if WordPerfect indicates that the
   document needs to be generated. This
   message usually indicates that the
   document was previously formatted for
   another printer.

6. Press **F7** (return to document) . . . .

20

DOCUMENT ON SCREEN

1. Press **Shift + F7** (Print) . . . .   `Shift` + `F7`

OR	Pull-down Menu	OR
A) Press **Alt + =**	`Alt` + `=`
B) Select **F** (File)	`F`
C) Select **P** (Print)	`P`

2. Select **one** of the following: **Option**

   a) **F** (Full Document) . . . .   `F`

   b) **P** (Page) . . . .   `P`

   c) **M** (Multiple Pages) . . . .   `M`

   Type page(s) with commas and dashes.

Examples:	-3	Pages 1-3
	2,5	Pages 2 and 5
	4-9	Pages 4-9
	6-	Pages 6 to last page
	-3, 8-10, 13	Pages 1-3, 8-10, 13

3. **Enter**   . . . .   `⏎`

   NOTE: *If printer location is set for manual feed, a beep or a message may appear. To start printing, issue a Go Command. (See Go Command — Start Printer on page 26.)*

   NOTE: *If WordPerfect indicates that the document needs to be generated type "y" or "n" as desired. This message indicates that the current document contains a list, table or an index that has not been updated.*

Printing (continued)

PRINT BLOCK

1. Place cursor on first character to be printed.

2. Press **Alt + F4** (Block) . . . . `Alt` + `F4`

OR	Pull-down Menu	OR
A) Press **Alt + =**		`Alt` + `=`
B) Select **E** (Edit)		`E`
C) Select **B** (Block)		`B`

3. Highlight text (see Block Text on page 10).

4. Press **Shift + F7** (Print) . . . . `Shift` + `F7`

OR	Pull-down Menu	OR
A) Press **Alt + =**		`Alt` + `=`
B) Select **F** (File)		`F`
C) Select **P** (Print)		`P`

5. Type **Y** (Print block)

 NOTE: Type "y" if WordPerfect indicates that the document needs to be generated. This message indicates that the current document contains a list, table or an index that has not been updated.

22

LIST FILES

1. Press **F5** (List Files) . . . . `F5`

OR	**Pull-down Menu**	OR
A) Press **Alt + =**		`Alt`+`≡`
B) Select **F** (File)		`F`
C) Select **F** (List Files)		`F`

> *NOTE: If necessary, change drive/directory to*
> *access files. Example: A:\DOCS*

2. **Enter** . . . . `↵`

3. Use cursor movement keys to highlight desired document.

4. Select **P** (Print) . . . . `P`

5. **Enter** (print entire document) . . . . `↵`

   OR   OR

   a) Type page(s) with commas and dashes.

   Examples:

-3	Pages 1-3
2,5	Pages 2 and 5
4-9	Pages 4-9
6-	Pages 6 to last page
-3, 8-10, 13	Pages 1-3, 8-10, 13

   b) **Enter** . . . . `↵`

   > *NOTE: Type "y" if WordPerfect indicates that the*
   > *document needs to be generated. This*
   > *message usually indicates that the*
   > *document was previously formatted for*
   > *another printer.*

6. Press **F7** (return to document) . . . . `F7`

CONTROL PRINTER

CANCEL PRINT JOB(S)

1. Press **Shift + F7** (Print) . . . . `Shift` + `F7`

OR	Pull-down Menu	OR
A) Press **Alt + =**		`Alt` + `=`
B) Select **F** (File)		`F`
C) Select **P** (Print)		`P`

2. Select **C** (Control Printer) . . . . `C`

3. Select **C** (Cancel Job[s]) . . . . `C`

4. Type job number to cancel . . . . Number

5. **Enter** (cancel print job) . . . . `↵`
   NOTE: Type "Y" or "C" to confirm if prompted.

6. Press **F7** (return to document) . . . . `F7`
   NOTE: Canceling a print request may not work if printer has a large buffer. See printer manual for details.

RUSH JOB

1. Press **Shift + F7** (Print) . . . . `Shift` + `F7`

OR	Pull-down Menu	OR
A) Press **Alt + =**		`Alt` + `=`
B) Select **F** (File)		`F`
C) Select **P** (Print)		`P`

2. Select **C** (Control Printer) . . . . `C`

3. Select **R** (Rush Job) . . . . `R`

4. Type job number to be placed ahead of all other print jobs . . . . Number

5. **Enter** . . . . `↵`

6. Press **F7** (return to document) . . . . `F7`

Control Printer (continued)

DISPLAY JOBS

1. Press **Shift + F7** (Print) . . . . `Shift`+`F7`

OR	Pull-down Menu	OR
A) Press **Alt + =**		`Alt`+`=`
B) Select **F** (File)		`F`
C) Select **P** (Print)		`P`

2. Select **C** (Control Printer) . . . . `C`

3. If four or more jobs:
   a) Select **D** (Display Job) . . . . `D`
   b) **Enter** . . . . `↵`

4. Press **F7** (return to document) . . . . `F7`

INTERRUPT AND RESUME PRINTING

1. Press **Shift + F7** (Print) . . . . `Shift`+`F7`

OR	Pull-down Menu	OR
A) Press **Alt + =**		`Alt`+`=`
B) Select **F** (File)		`F`
C) Select **P** (Print)		`P`

2. Select **C** (Control Printer) . . . . `C`

3. Select **S** (Stop) . . . . `S`
   NOTE: Type "Y" to confirm if prompted.
4. Make any necessary changes to printer.

Continued ...

Control Printer (continued)
Interrupt and Resume Printing (continued)

5. Select **G** (Go - Start Printer) .... `G`

   Enter .... `↵`

   OR   OR

   Type starting page number and
   resume printing .... Number

6. Press **F7** (return to document) .... `F7`

VIEW DOCUMENT ON SCREEN

*NOTE: Displays a document as it would appear
   in printed form. A graphics card is
   necessary for this feature.*

1. Press **Shift + F7** (Print) .... `Shift`+`F7`

OR	Pull-down Menu	OR
A) Press **Alt + =**		`Alt`+`≡`
B) Select **F** (File)		`F`
C) Select **P** (Print)		`P`

2. Select **V** (View Document) .... `V`

3. Select **one** of the following: Option

   a) **1** (100%) .... `1`

   b) **2** (200%) .... `2`

   c) **3** (Full Page) .... `3`

   d) **4** (Facing Pages) .... `4`

4. Press **F7** (return to document) .... `F7`

26
PRINTING SPECIAL OPTIONS

SELECT PRINTER

1. Press **Shift + F7** (Print) . . . . `Shift`+`F7`

OR	Pull-down Menu	OR
A) Press **Alt + =**		`Alt`+`=`
B) Select **F** (File)		`F`
C) Select **P** (Print)		`P`

2. Select **S** (Select Printer) . . . . `S`

3. Use cursor movement keys to highlight desired printer.

   NOTE: If desired printer is not listed, see Additional Printer on page 27.

4. Select **S** (Select) . . . . `S`

5. Press **F7** (return to document) . . . . `F7`

GO COMMAND — START PRINTER

NOTE: Use this command to start printing a document when the paper type location is set to manual feed.

1. Press **Shift + F7** (Print) . . . . `Shift`+`F7`

OR	Pull-down Menu	OR
A) Press **Alt + =**		`Alt`+`=`
B) Select **F** (File)		`F`
C) Select **P** (Print)		`P`

2. Select **C** (Control Printer) . . . . `C`

3. Select **G** (Go - Startp Printer) . . . . `G`

4. Press **F7** (return to document) . . . . `F7`

Printing Special Options (continued)

ADDITIONAL PRINTER

1. Press **Shift + F7** (Print) . . . . **Shift** + **F7**

OR	Pull-down Menu	OR
A) Press **Alt + =**		**Alt** + **=**
B) Select **F** (File)		**F**
C) Select **P** (Print)		**P**

2. Select **S** (Select Printer) . . . . **S**

3. Select **A** (Additional Printers) . . . . **A**

4. Use cursor movement keys to highlight desired printer.

   NOTE: If printer is not listed, run installation program again to copy additional printer files.

5. Select **S** (Select) . . . . **S**

6. **Enter** . . . . **↵**

7. Press **F7** (exit Printer file) **F7**

8. Press **F7** (exit Select Print: Edit) **F7**

9. Press **F7** (exit Select Printer) **F7**

10. Press **F7** (return to document) **F7**

28

Printing Special Options (continued)

EDIT (Printer File)

1. Press **Shift + F7** (Print) . . . . `Shift` + `F7`

OR	Pull-down Menu	OR
A) Press **Alt + =**		`Alt` + `=`
B) Select **F** (File)	. . . . .	`F`
C) Select **P** (Print)		`P`

2. Select **S** (Select Printer) . . . . `S`

3. Select **E** (Edit) . . . . `E`

4. Select **N** (Name) . . . . `N`

   a) Type printer name if different from default name.

   b) **Enter** . . . . `↵`

5. Select **P** (Port) . . . . `P`

   a) Select desired printer port.

   b) **Enter** . . . . `↵`

6. Select **S** (Sheet Feeder) . . . . `S`

   a) Use cursor movement keys to highlight desired feeder.

   b) Select **S** (Select) . . . . `S`

   c) Press **F7** . . . . `F7`

NOTE: If soft fonts are used, a path must be specified. Refer to your WordPerfect user manual for details.

Continued ...

Printing Special Options (continued)
EDIT (Printer File continued)

7. Select **F** (Initial Base Font) . . . . 🄵

   a) Use cursor movement keys to highlight desired base font.

   b) Select **S** (Select) . . . . 🅂

8. Press **F7** (exit Select Printer: Edit) . . . . 🄵🄾

9. Press **F7** (exit Print: Select Printer) . . . . 🄵🄾

10. Press **F7** (return to document) . . . . 🄵🄾

BINDING OFFSET

1. Press **Shift + F7** (Print) . . . . 🅂🄷🄸🄵🅃 + 🄵🄾

OR	Pull-down Menu	OR
A) Press **Alt + =**		🄰🄻🅃 + 🄴
B) Select **F** (File)		🄵
C) Select **P** (Print)		🄿

2. Select **B** (Binding Offset) . . . . 🄱

3. Type number of inches document should be offset for binding purposes . . . . Number

4. **Enter** . . . . ⏎

5. Press **F7** (return to document) . . . . 🄵🄾

30

Printing Special Options (continued)

NUMBER OF COPIES

1. Press **Shift + F7** (Print) . . . . `Shift`+`F7`

OR	Pull-down Menu	OR
A) Press **Alt + =**		`Alt`+`=`
B) Select **F** (File)		`F`
C) Select **P** (Print)		`P`

2. Select **N** (Number of Copies) . . . . `N`

3. Type number of copies to be printed . . . . . Number

4. **Enter** . . . . `↵`

5. Press **F7** (return to document) . . . . `F7`

MULTIPLE COPIES GENERATED BY
If supported by your printer, selecting "Printer" will speed up printing of multiple copies, especially if the the current print job contains graphics or soft fonts.

1. Press **Shift + F7** (Print) . . . . `Shift`+`F7`

OR	Pull-down Menu	OR
A) Press **Alt + =**		`Alt`+`=`
B) Select **F** (File)		`F`
C) Select **P** (Print)		`P`

2. Select **U** (Multiple Copies Generated By) . . . . . `U`

3. Select **one** of the following: Option

   a) **W** (WordPerfect) . . . . `W`

   b) **P** (Printer) . . . . `P`

   c) **N** (Network) . . . . `N`

4. Press **F7** (return to document) . . . . `F7`

Printing Special Options (continued)

GRAPHICS QUALITY
1. Press **Shift + F7** (Print) . . . . `Shift` + `F7`

OR	Pull-down Menu	OR
A) Press **Alt + =**		`Alt` + `=`
B) Select **F** (File)		`F`
C) Select **P** (Print)		`P`

2. Select **G** (Graphics Quality) . . . . `G`
3. Select **one** of the following: Option
   a) **N** (Do Not Print) . . . . `N`
   b) **D** (Draft) . . . . `D`
   c) **M** (Medium) . . . . `M`
   d) **H** (High) . . . . `H`
4. Press **F7** (return to document) . . . . `F7`

TEXT QUALITY
1. Press **Shift + F7** (Print) . . . . `Shift` + `F7`

OR	Pull-down Menu	OR
A) Press **Alt + =**		`Alt` + `=`
B) Select **F** (File)		`F`
C) Select **P** (Print)		`P`

2. Select **T** (Text Quality) . . . . `T`

Continued ...

Printing Special Options (continued)
Text Quality (continued)

3. Select **one** of the following: Option

   a) **N** (Do Not Print) . . . . ▨N

   b) **D** (Draft) . . . . ▨D

   c) **M** (Medium) . . . . ▨M

   d) **H** (High) . . . . ▨H

4. Press **F7** (return to document) . . . . ▨F7

DOCUMENT ASSEMBLY

BOILERPLATE TEXT

1. Clear Screen (see Clear Screen on page 8).

2. Type text for Boilerplate.

3. Press **F7** (Exit) . . . . ▨F7

OR	Pull-down Menu	OR
A) Press **Alt** + = ...		▨Alt + ▨=
B) Select **F** (File)		▨F
C) Select **S** (Save)		▨S

4. **Enter** (save document) . . . . ▨⏎

5. Type name of Boilerplate document . . . . . Filename

6. **Enter** . . . . ▨⏎

7. **Enter** (exit to new document screen) . . . . ▨⏎

Document Assembly (continued)

COMBINING DOCUMENTS

1. Press **Shift + F10** (Retrieve) ...... **Shift** + **F10**

OR	Pull-down Menu	OR
A) Press **Alt + =**		**Alt** + **=**
B) Select **F** (File)		**F**
C) Select **R** (Retrieve)		**R**
---

2. Type name of document that will be combined with Boilerplate document .... Filename

3. **Enter** .... **⏎**

4. Place cursor where Boilerplate will be inserted.

5. Press **Shift + F10** (Retrieve) ...... **Shift** + **F10**

OR	Pull-down Menu	OR
A) Press **Alt + =**		**Alt** + **=**
B) Select **F** (File)		**F**
C) Select **R** (Retrieve)		**R**
---

6. Type name of Boilerplate document ..... Filename

7. **Enter** .... **⏎**

8. Repeat steps 4-7 for each Boilerplate to be placed.

MARGINS

SETTING LEFT AND RIGHT MARGINS

1. Place cursor at beginning of line where margin change is to begin.

2. Press **Shift + F8** (Format) .... `Shift`+`F8`

OR	Pull-down Menu	OR
A) Press **Alt + =**		`Alt`+`=`
B) Select **L** (Layout)		`L`

---

3. Select **L** (Line) .... `L`

4. Select **M** (Margin) .... `M`
   NOTE: Margins are expressed in inches.

5. Type Left Margin .... Number

6. Enter .... `↵`

7. Type Right Margin .... Number

8. Enter .... `↵`

9. Press **F7** (return to document) .... `F7`

SETTING TOP AND BOTTOM MARGIN

1. Place cursor at top of page.

2. Press **Shift + F8** (Format) .... `Shift`+`F8`

OR	Pull-down Menu	OR
A) Press **Alt + =**		`Alt`+`=`
B) Select **L** (Layout)		`L`

---

3. Select **P** (Page) .... `P`

4. Select **M** (Margin) .... `M`
   NOTE: Margins are expressed in inches.

Continued ...

Margins (continued)
Setting Top and Bottom Margin (continued)

5. Type Top Margin .... Number

6. **Enter** .... ⏎

7. Type Bottom Margin .... Number

8. **Enter** .... ⏎

9. Press **F7** (return to document) F7

MARGIN RELEASE

NOTE: Margin release moves cursor to previous tab setting.

1. Place cursor at left margin of line where margin is to be released.

2. Press **Shift + Tab** (Margin Release). Shift + Tab

OR	Pull-down Menu	OR
A) Press **Alt + =**		Alt + =
B) Select **L** (Layout)		L
C) Select **A** (Align)		A
D) Select **M** (Margin Rel)		M

36
TAB SET

NORMAL STYLE (Left-Justified)

1. Place cursor on line where tab change is to begin.

2. Press **Shift + F8** (Format) .... **Shift** + **F8**

OR	**Pull-down Menu**	OR
A) Press **Alt + =**		**Alt** + **=**
B) Select **L** (Layout)		**L**

3. Select **L** (Line) .... **L**

4. Select **T** (Tabs) .... **T**

5. Press **Home, Home, Left Arrow** .... **Home** **Home** **←**

6. Press **Ctrl + End** (clear all tabs) .... **Ctrl** + **End**

7. Mark tab settings:

   a) Place cursor at desired tab setting.

   b) Type **L** .... **L**

   OR   **OR**

   a) Type tab position .... Number

   b) **Enter** .... **↵**

   NOTE: A tab can be deleted by moving the cursor under (L) and pressing Delete.

8. Repeat step 7 for additional tabs.

9. Press **F7** **F7**

10. Press **F7** (return to document) **F7**

Continued ...

37

Tab Set (continued)

SPECIAL TAB STYLES

1. Place cursor on line where tab change is to begin.

2. Press **Shift + F8** (Format) . . . . `Shift + F8`

OR	Pull-down Menu	OR
A) Press **Alt + =**		`Alt + =`
B) Select **L** (Layout)		`L`

3. Select **L** (Line) . . . . `L`

4. Select **T** (Tabs) . . . . `T`

5. Press **Home, Home, Left Arrow** . . . . `Home` `Home` `←`

6. Press **Ctrl + End** (clear all tabs) . . . . `Ctrl + End`

7. Place cursor at desired tab setting.

8. Select **one** of the following: Option

   a) **L** (Left justify text [default setting]) . . . . `L`

   b) **R** (Right justify text) . . . . `R`

   c) **D** (Decimal align text) . . . . `D`

   d) **C** (Center text) . . . . `C`

   NOTE: Type a period (.) over the letter for those tabs that require a dot leader. They will be displayed in reverse video.

9. Repeat steps **7** and **8** for additional tabs.

   NOTE: A tab can be deleted by moving the cursor under tab style and pressing Delete.

10. Press **F7** . . . . `F7`

11. Press **F7** (return to document) . . . . `F7`

Tab Set (continued)

MULTIPLE TABS SET
AT REPEATED INTERVALS

1. Press **Shift + F8** (Format) . . . . `Shift` + `F8`

OR	Pull-down Menu	OR
A) Press **Alt + =**		`Alt` + `=`
B) Select **L** (Layout)		`L`

2. Select **L** (Line format) . . . . `L`

3. Select **T** (Tab Set) . . . . `T`

4. Press **Home, Home,
   Left Arrow** . . . . `Home` `Home` `←`

5. Press **Ctrl + End** (clear all tabs) . . . . `Ctrl` + `End`

6. Type position number of first tab. . . . . Number

7. **Enter** . . . . `⏎`

8. Type letter of tab style. . . . . Letter
   NOTE: See Special tab styles section.

9. Type position number of first tab (again) . . Number

10. Type comma (,) . . . . `,`

11. Type number of spaces between tabs. . . . . Number
    *Example: 0,.5 (Will set tabs at every .5 inches
    beginning at position zero.)*

12. **Enter** (set tab intervals) . . . . `⏎`
    *NOTE: A tab can be deleted by moving the
    cursor under tab style and pressing Delete.*

13. Press **F7** . . . . `F7`

14. Press **F7** (return to document) . . . . `F7`

Tab Set (continued)

TAB ALIGN

VERTICALLY LINE UP TEXT OR NUMBERS

1. Press **Ctrl + F6** (Tab Align) .... `Ctrl`+`F6`

OR	Pull-down Menu	OR
A) Press **Alt + =**		`Alt`+`=`
B) Select **L** (Layout)		`L`
C) Select **A** (Align)		`A`
D) Select **T** (Tab Align)		`T`

2. Type text to be aligned.

   NOTE: The default Align Character is the period (.).

SELECTING SPECIAL ALIGN CHARACTER

1. Press **Shift + F8** (Format) .... `Shift`+`F8`

OR	Pull-down Menu	OR
A) Press **Alt + =**		`Alt`+`=`
B) Select **L** (Layout)		`L`

2. Select **O** (Other) .... `O`

3. Select **D** (Decimal/Align Character) .... `D`

4. Type alignment character. .... Character

5. **Enter** .... `↵`

6. Press **F7** (return to document) .... `F7`

40

INDENT

NOTE: Tab settings determine indent positions.

INDENT FIRST LINE (From Left Margin)

New paragraph

1. Place cursor at beginning of line.

2. Press **Tab** (until cursor is at desired position).

3. Type paragraph.

4. **Enter** (end indent) . . . .

Existing paragraph

1. Place cursor on first character of paragraph.

2. Press **Tab** (until cursor is at desired position).

INDENT EVERY LINE OF PARAGRAPH (From Left Margin)

New Paragraph

Note: This feature sets a temporary left margin.

1. Place cursor at beginning of line.

2. Press **F4** (Indent [until cursor is at desired position])) . . . .

OR	**Pull-down Menu**	OR
A) Press **Alt + =**		**Alt** + **▤**
B) Select **L** (Layout)		**L**
C) Select **A** (Align)		**A**
D) Select **I** (Indent)		**I**

NOTE: Repeat steps A-D until cursor is at desired tab position.

3. Type paragraph.

4. **Enter** (end indent) . . . .

Indent (continued)
Indent Every Line Of Paragraph (From Left Margin, continued)

Existing Paragraph

1. Place cursor on first character of paragraph.

2. Press **F4** (Indent [until cursor is at
   desired position]) . . . .

OR	Pull-down Menu	OR
A) Press **Alt + =**		Alt + =
B) Select **L** (Layout)		L
C) Select **A** (Align)		A
D) Select **I** (Indent)		I

> *NOTE: Repeat steps A-D until cursor is at desired*
> *tab position.*

3. Press **Down Arrow** until remaining lines
   are indented . . . .

4. **Enter** (end L/R indent) . . . .

LEFT/RIGHT INDENT

New paragraph

1. Place cursor at beginning of line.

2. Press **Shift + F4** (Indent L/R [until
   cursor is at desired position]) . . . . . . **Shift + F4**

OR	Pull-down Menu	OR
A) Press **Alt + =**		Alt + =
B) Select **L** (Layout)		L
C) Select **A** (Align)		A
D) Select **N** (Indent)		N

> *NOTE: Repeat steps A-D until cursor is at desired*
> *tab position.*

Continued ...

Indent (continued)
Left/Right Indent (continued)

3. Type paragraph.

4. **Enter** (end indent) . . . .

Existing Paragraph
1. Place cursor on first character of paragraph.

2. Press **Shift + F4** (Indent L/R [until
   cursor is at desired position]) . . . . . . Shift + F4

OR	Pull-down Menu	OR
A) Press **Alt + =**		Alt + =
B) Select **L** (Layout)		L
C) Select **A** (Align)		A
D) Select **N** (Indent)		N

NOTE: Repeat steps A-D until cursor is at desired
       tab position.

3. Press **Down Arrow** until remaining lines
   are indented. . . . .

4. **Enter** (end indent) . . . .

Indent (continued)

HANGING INDENT

New paragraph

1. Place cursor at beginning of line.

2. Press **F4** (Indent [until cursor is at
   desired position]) . . . . `F4`

OR	Pull-down Menu	OR
A) Press **Alt + =**		`Alt`+`=`
B) Select **L** (Layout)		`L`
C) Select **A** (Align)		`A`
D) Select **I** (Indent)		`I`

> *NOTE: Repeat steps A-D until cursor is at desired
> tab position.*

3. Press **Shift + Tab** (Margin Release). `Shift`+`Tab`

OR	Pull-down Menu	OR
A) Press **Alt + =**		`Alt`+`=`
B) Select **L** (Layout)		`L`
C) Select **A** (Align)		`A`
D) Select **M** (Margin Rel)		`M`

4. Type paragraph.

5. **Enter** (end hanging indent) . . . .

44

Indent (continued)
Hanging Indent (continued)

Existing Paragraph
  1. Place cursor on first character of paragraph.

  2. Press **F4** (Indent [until cursor is at
     desired tab position]) . . . . `F4`

OR	Pull-down Menu	OR
A) Press **Alt + =**		`Alt`+`=`
B) Select **L** (Layout)		`L`
C) Select **A** (Align)		`A`
D) Select **I** (Indent)		`I`

> *NOTE: Repeat steps A-D until cursor is at desired
>   tab position.*

  3. Press **Shift + Tab** (Margin Release). `Shift`+`Tab`

OR	Pull-down Menu	OR
A) Press **Alt + =**		`Alt`+`=`
B) Select **L** (Layout)		`L`
C) Select **A** (Align)		`A`
D) Select **M** (Margin Rel)		`M`

  4. Press **Down Arrow** until remaining lines
     are indented . . . .

LINE SPACING

1. Place cursor on line where spacing change is to begin.

2. Press **Shift + F8** (Format) . . . . **Shift**+**F8**

OR	**Pull-down Menu**	OR
A) Press **Alt + =**		**Alt**+**=**
B) Select **L** (Layout)		**L**

3. Select **L** (Line) . . . . **L**

4. Select **S** (Line **S**pacing) . . . . **S**

5. Type spacing . . . . Number
   Examples: 1.5 = One and one-half Space
   2 = Double Space
   3 = Triple Space

6. **Enter** . . . .

7. Press **F7** (return to document) **F7**

CENTERING TEXT

BEFORE TYPING TEXT

1. Place cursor at beginning of line.

2. Press **Shift + F6** (Center) . . . . **Shift**+**F6**

OR	**Pull-down Menu**	OR
A) Press **Alt + =**		**Alt**+**=**
B) Select **L** (Layout)		**L**
C) Select **A** (Align)		**A**
D) Select **C** (Center)		**C**

3. Type text (maximum of one line).

4. **Enter** . . . .

5. Repeat steps 1-4 for additional lines.

46

Centering Text (continued)

EXISTING TEXT

> *NOTE: There must be a hard return at the end of line that will be centered.*

1. Place cursor at beginning of line to be centered.

2. Press **Shift + F6** (Center) . . . . **Shift** + **F6**

OR	Pull-down Menu	OR
A) Press **Alt + =**		**Alt** + **=**
B) Select **L** (Layout)		**L**
C) Select **A** (Align)		**A**
D) Select **C** (Center)		**C**

3. Press **Down Arrow** . . . . **↓**

BLOCK OF TEXT

1. Place cursor at beginning of line to be centered.

2. Press **Alt + F4** (Block) . . . . **Alt** + **F4**

OR	Pull-down Menu	OR
A) Press **Alt + =**		**Alt** + **=**
B) Select **E** (Edit)		**E**
C) Select **B** (Block)		**B**

3. Highlight text (see Block Text on page 10).

4. Press **Shift + F6** (Center) . . . . **Shift** + **F6**

OR	Pull-down Menu	OR
A) Press **Alt + =**		**Alt** + **=**
B) Select **L** (Layout)		**L**
C) Select **A** (Align)		**A**
D) Select **C** (Center)		**C**

5. Type **Y** (center highlighted text) . . . . **Y**

Centering Text (continued)

CENTER PAGE (Top to Bottom)

1. Place cursor at top of page.

2. Press **Shift + F8** (Format) .... **Shift** + **F8**

OR	Pull-down Menu	OR
A) Press **Alt + =**		**Alt** + **=**
B) Select **L** (Layout)		**L**

3. Select **P** (Page) .... **P**

4. Select **C** (Center page top to bottom) .... **C**

5. Type **Y** (to Center Page) .... **Y**

6. **Enter** .... **⏎**

7. Press **F7** (return to document) **F7**
   NOTE: The page will not appear centered on the screen, but will print with text centered.

CENTER A HEADING IN A COLUMN

1. Place cursor at beginning of column.

2. Press **Shift + F6** (Center) .... **Shift** + **F6**

OR	Pull-down Menu	OR
A) Press **Alt + =**		**Alt** + **=**
B) Select **L** (Layout)		**L**
C) Select **A** (Align)		**A**
D) Select **C** (Center)		**C**

3. Type text.

4. **Enter** .... **⏎**

48
CENTER JUSTIFICATION

BEFORE TYPING TEXT

1. Place cursor on line where text centering is to begin.

2. Press **Shift + F8** (Format) .... `Shift`+`F8`

OR	Pull-down Menu	OR
A) Press **Alt + =**		`Alt`+`=`
B) Select **L** (Layout)		`L`

3. Select **L** (Line) .... `L`

4. Select **J** (Justification) .... `J`

5. Select **one** of the following: Option

   a) **L** (Left) .... `L`

   b) **C** (Center) .... `C`

   c) **R** (Right) .... `R`

   d) **F** (Full) .... `F`

6. Press **F7** (return to document) .... `F7`

7. Type Text.

JUSTIFICATION

1. Place cursor on line where justification change is to begin.

2. Press **Shift + F8** (Format) . . . . **Shift** + **F8**

3. Select **L** (Line) . . . . **L**

4. Select **J** (Justification) . . . . **J**

5. Select **one** of the following: **Option**

   a) **L** (Left) . . . . **L**

   b) **C** (Center) . . . . **C**

   c) **R** (Right) . . . . **R**

   d) **F** (Full) . . . . **F**

6. Press **F7** (return to document) **F7**

OR	Pull-down Menu	OR

1. Place cursor where justification change is to begin.

2. Press **Alt + =** . . . . **Alt** + **=**

3. Select **L** (Layout) . . . . **L**

4. Select **J** (Justify) . . . . **J**

5. Select **one** of the following: **Option**

   a) **L** (Left) . . . . **L**

   b) **C** (Center) . . . . **C**

   c) **R** (Right) . . . . **R**

   d) **F** (Full) . . . . **F**

50
UNDERLINING TEXT

BEFORE TYPING TEXT

1. Press **F8** (Underline) . . . . `F8`

OR	Pull-down Menu	OR
A) Press **Alt + =**		`Alt`+`=`
B) Select **O** (Font)		`O`
C) Select **A** (Appearance)		`A`
D) Select **U** (Underline)		`U`

2. Type text.

3. Press **F8** (Underline off) . . . . `F8`

OR	Pull-down Menu	OR
A) Press **Alt + =**		`Alt`+`=`
B) Select **O** (Font)		`O`
C) Select **A** (Appearance)		`A`
D) Select **U** (Underline)		`U`

EXISTING TEXT

1. Place cursor on first character of text to be underlined.

2. Press **Alt + F4** (Block) . . . . `Alt`+`F4`

OR	Pull-down Menu	OR
A) Press **Alt + =**		`Alt`+`=`
B) Select **E** (Edit)		`E`
C) Select **B** (Block)		`B`

3. Highlight text (See Block Text on page 10).

51

Underline Text (continued)
Existing Text (continued)

4. Press **F8** (Underline) .... `F8`

OR	Pull-down Menu	OR
A) Press **Alt + =**		`Alt`+`=`
B) Select **O** (Font)		`O`
C) Select **A** (Appearance)		`A`
D) Select **U** (Underline)		`U`

DOUBLE UNDERLINE NEW TEXT

1. Press **Ctrl + F8** (Font) .... `Ctrl`+`F8`

OR	Pull-down Menu	OR
A) Press **Alt + =**		`Alt`+`=`
B) Select **O** (Font)		`O`

2. Select **A** (Appearance) .... `A`
3. Select **D** (Dbl Und) .... `D`
4. Type Text.
   NOTE: Double Underline will not be shown on the screen, but will appear in the document when it is printed. See View Document on Screen on page 25 to view double underline.
5. Press **Right Arrow** (to end Double Underline).

Underline Text (continued)

DOUBLE UNDERLINE EXISTING TEXT

1. Place cursor on first character of text to be underlined.

2. Press **Alt + F4** (Block) . . . . `Alt`+`F4`

OR	Pull-down Menu	OR
A) Press **Alt + =**		`Alt`+`=`
B) Select **E** (Edit)		`E`
C) Select **B** (Block)		`B`

3. Highlight text (See Block Text on page 10).

4. Press **Ctrl + F8** (Font) . . . . `Ctrl`+`F8`

OR	Pull-down Menu	OR
A) Press **Alt + =**		`Alt`+`=`
B) Select **O** (Font)		`O`

5. Select **A** (Appearance) . . . . `A`

6. Select **D** (Dbl Und) . . . . `D`

Underline Text (continued)

UNDERLINING SPACES/TABS

1. Press **Shift + F8** (Format) . . . . | **Shift** + **F8** |

OR	Pull-down Menu	OR
A) Press **Alt + =**		**Alt** + **=**
B) Select **L** (Layout)		**L**

2. Select **O** (Other) . . . . **O**

3. Select **U** (Underline) . . . . **U**

4. Type **Y** (underline spaces) . . . . **Y**

   OR   OR

   Type **N** (do not underline spaces) . . . . **N**

5. Type **Y** (underline tabs) . . . . **Y**

   OR   OR

   Type **N** (do not underline tabs) . . . . **N**

6. Press **F7** (return to document) **F7**

54
FLUSH RIGHT

BEFORE TYPING TEXT

1. Press **Alt + F6** (Flush Right) . . . . `Alt`+`F6`

OR	Pull-down Menu	OR
A) Press **Alt + =**		`Alt`+`=`
B) Select **L** (Layout)		`L`
C) Select **A** (Align)		`A`
D) Select **F** (Flush right)		`F`

2. Type text (maximum of one line).

3. **Enter** . . . . `⏎`

4. Repeat steps 1-3 for additional lines.

EXISTING TEXT

> *NOTE: A hard return must be inserted at the end of a flush right line or paragraph.*

1. Place cursor at left margin.

2. Press **Alt + F4** (Block) . . . . `Alt`+`F4`

OR	Pull-down Menu	OR
A) Press **Alt + =**		`Alt`+`=`
B) Select **E** (Edit)		`E`
C) Select **B** (Block)		`B`

3. Highlight text (See Block Text on page 10).

Continued ...

Flush Right (continued)
Existing Text (continued)

4. Press **Alt + F6** (Flush Right) . . . . `Alt`+`F6`

OR	Pull-down Menu	OR
A) Press **Alt + =**		`Alt`+`=`
B) Select **L** (Layout)		`L`
C) Select **A** (Align)		`A`
D) Select **F** (Flush right)		`F`

5. Press **Down Arrow** . . . . `↓`

BOLDING TEXT

BEFORE TYPING TEXT

1. Press **F6** (Bold) . . . . `F6`

OR	Pull-down Menu	OR
A) Press **Alt + =**		`Alt`+`=`
B) Select **O** (Font)		`O`
C) Select **A** (Appearance)		`A`
D) Select **B** (Bold)		`B`

2. Type text.

3. Press **F6** (Bold) . . . . `F6`

OR	Pull-down Menu	OR
A) Press **Alt + =**		`Alt`+`=`
B) Select **O** (Font)		`O`
C) Select **A** (Appearance)		`A`
D) Select **B** (Bold)		`B`

EXISTING TEXT

1. Place cursor on first character of text to be bolded.

2. Press **Alt** + **F4** (Block) . . . . `Alt`+`F4`

OR	Pull-down Menu	OR
A) Press **Alt** + **=**		`Alt`+`=`
B) Select **E** (Edit)		`E`
C) Select **B** (Block)		`B`

3. Highlight text (See Block Text on page 10).

4. Press **F6** (Bold) . . . . `F6`

OR	Pull-down Menu	OR
A) Press **Alt** + **=**		`Alt`+`=`
B) Select **O** (Font)		`O`
C) Select **A** (Appearance)		`A`
D) Select **B** (Bold)		`B`

MOVE AND COPY TEXT

BLOCK OF TEXT

1. Place cursor on first character of text to be moved or copied.

2. Press **Alt + F4** (Block) . . . . `Alt`+`F4`

OR	Pull-down Menu	OR
A) Press **Alt + =**		`Alt`+`=`
B) Select **E** (Edit)		`E`
C) Select **B** (Block)		`B`

3. Highlight text (See Block Text on page 10).

4. Press **Ctrl + F4, B** (Move Block) `Ctrl`+`F4` `B`

OR	Pull-down Menu	OR
A) Press **Alt + =**		`Alt`+`=`
B) Select **E** (Edit)		`E`

5. Select **M** (Move) . . . . `M`

   OR   OR

   Select **C** (Copy) . . . . `C`

6. Place cursor where text is to be moved or copied.

7. **Enter** . . . . `⏎`

Move or Copy Text (continued)

SENTENCE/PARAGRAPH/PAGE

1. Place cursor on first character of text to be moved or copied.

2. Press **Ctrl + F4** (Move) .... `Ctrl` + `F4`

OR	Pull-down Menu	OR
A) Press **Alt + =**		`Alt` + `=`
B) Select **E** (Edit)		`E`
C) Select **E** (Select)		`E`

3. Select **one** of the following: Option

   a) **S** (Sentence) .... `S`

   b) **P** (Paragraph) .... `P`

   c) **A** (Page) .... `A`

4. Select **M** (Move) .... `M`

   OR   OR

   Select **C** (Copy) .... `C`

5. Place cursor where text is to be moved or copied.

6. **Enter** .... `↵`

Move or Copy Text (continued)

TABULAR COLUMN/RECTANGULAR BLOCK OF TEXT

1. Place cursor on first character of text to be moved or copied.

2. Press **Alt + F4** (Block) . . . . **Alt**+**F4**

OR	Pull-down Menu	OR
A) Press **Alt + =**		**Alt**+**=**
B) Select **E** (Edit)		**E**
C) Select **B** (Block)		**B**

3. Highlight text (See Block Text on page 10).

4. Press **Ctrl + F4** (Move) . . . . **Ctrl**+**F4**

OR	Pull-down Menu	OR
A) Press **Alt + =**		**Alt**+**=**
B) Select **E** (Edit)		**E**
C) Select **E** (Select)		**E**

5. Select **C** (Tabular Column) . . . . **C**

 OR OR

 Select **R** (Rectangle) . . . . **R**

6. Select **M** (Move) . . . . **M**

 OR OR

 Select **C** (Copy) . . . . **C**

60

APPEND

Add a block of text to the end of an existing document.

1. Place cursor on first character of text to be appended.

2. Press **Alt + F4** (Block) . . . . `Alt`+`F4`

OR	Pull-down Menu	OR
A) Press **Alt + =**		`Alt`+`=`
B) Select **E** (Edit)		`E`
C) Select **B** (Block)		`B`

3. Highlight text (See Block Text on page 10).

4. Press **Ctrl + F4** (Move) . . . . `Ctrl`+`F4`

5. Select **B** (Block) . . . . `B`

OR	Pull-down Menu	OR
A) Press **Alt + =**		`Alt`+`=`
B) Select **E** (Edit)		`E`

6. Select **A** (Append) . . . . `A`

7. Type name of document to which block will
   be appended . . . . Filename

8. **Enter** . . . . `↵`

PAPER SIZE/TYPE

SELECT

1. Place cursor at top of page.

2. Press **Shift + F8** (Format) . . . . `Shift`+`F8`

OR	Pull-down Menu	OR
A) Press **Alt + =**		`Alt`+`=`
B) Select **L** (Layout)		`L`

3. Select **P** (Page) . . . . `P`

4. Select **S** (Paper Size) . . . . `S`

5. Use cursor movement keys to highlight desired paper definition.

6. Select **S** (Select) . . . . `S`

7. Press **F7** (return to document) . . . . `F7`

62

Paper Size/Type (continued)

ADD

1. Place cursor at top of page.
2. Press **Shift + F8** (Format) . . . . `Shift` + `F8`

OR	Pull-down Menu	OR
A) Press **Alt + =**		`Alt` + `=`
B) Select **L** (Layout)		`L`

3. Select **P** (Page) . . . . `P`
4. Select **S** (Paper Size) . . . . `S`
5. Select **A** (Add) . . . . `A`
6. Select **one** of the following: **Option**
   - a) **S** (Standard) . . . . `S`
   - b) **B** (Bond) . . . . `B`
   - c) **H** (Letterhead) . . . . `H`
   - d) **L** (Labels) . . . . `L`
   - e) **E** (Envelope) . . . . `E`
   - f) **T** (Transparency) . . . . `T`
   - g) **C** (Cardstock) . . . . `C`
   - h) **A** (ALL OTHERS) . . . . `A`
   - i) **O** (Other) . . . . `O`
7. Select **S** (Paper Size) . . . . `S`

Continued ...

Paper Size/Type (continued)
Add (continued)

8. Select **one** of the following: Option

   a) **S** (Standard) 8.5" x 11" . . . .   S

   b) **T** (standard Landscape) 11" x 8.5" . . . .   T

   c) **L** (Legal) 8.5" x 14"   L

   d) **G** (Legal Landscape) 14" x 8.5" . . . .   G

   e) **E** (Envelope) 9.5" x 4" . . . .   E

   f) **H** (Half Sheet) 5.5" x 8.5" . . . .   H

   g) **U** (US Government) 8" x 11" . . . .   U

   h) **A** (A4) 210mm x 297mm . . . .   A

   i) **N** (A4 Landscape) 297mm x 210mm . . .   N

   j) **O** (Other) . . . .   O

9. Press **F7** F7

10. Press **F7** F7

11. Press **F7** (return to document) F7

64

Paper Size/Type (continued)
EDIT

1. Place cursor at top of page.
2. Press **Shift + F8** (Format) . . . . `Shift` + `F8`

OR	**Pull-down Menu**	OR
A) Press **Alt + ≡**		`Alt` + `≡`
B) Select **L** (Layout)		`L`

---

3. Select **P** (Page) . . . . `P`
4. Select **S** (Paper Size) . . . . `S`

5. Use cursor movement keys to highlight desired paper definition.
6. Select **E** (Edit) . . . . `E`
7. Select **S** (Paper Size) . . . . `S`

8. Select **one** of the following: **Option**

  a) **S** (Standard) 8.5" x 11" . . . . `S`

  b) **T** (standard Landscape) 11" x 8.5" . . . . `T`

  c) **L** (Legal) 8.5" x 14" . . . . `L`

  d) **G** (Legal Landscape) 14" x 8.5" . . . . `G`

  e) **E** (Envelope) 9.5" x 4" . . . . `E`

  f) **H** (Half Sheet) 5.5" x 8.5" . . . . `H`

  g) **U** (US Government) 8" x 11" . . . . `U`

  h) **A** (A4) 210mm x 297mm . . . . `A`

  i) **N** (A4 Landscape) 297mm x 210mm . . . `N`

  j) **O** (Other) . . . . `O`

Continued ...

Paper Size/Type (continued)
Edit (continued)

9. Select **T** (Paper Type) . . . . `T`

10. Select **one** of the following: Option

   a) **S** (Standard) . . . . `S`

   b) **B** (Bond) . . . . `B`

   c) **H** (Letterhead) . . . . `H`

   d) **L** (Labels) . . . . `L`

   e) **E** (Envelope) . . . . `E`

   f) **T** (Transparency) . . . . `T`

   g) **C** (Cardstock) . . . . `C`

   h) **A** (ALL OTHERS) . . . . `A`

   i) **O** (Other) . . . . `O`

11. Press **F7** . . . . `F7`

12. Press **F7** . . . . `F7`

13. Press **F7** (return to document) . . . . `F7`

PAGE NUMBERING

1. Place cursor at top of page to be numbered.

2. Press **Shift + F8** (Format) . . . . **Shift** + **F8**

OR	**Pull-down Menu**	OR
A) Press **Alt + =**		**Alt** + **=**
B) Select **L** (Layout)		**L**

3. Select **P** (Page) . . . . **P**

4. Select **N** (Page **N**umbering) . . . . **N**

5. Select **P** (Page Number **P**osition) . . . . **P**

6. Select **one** of the following: **Option**

    a) **1** (Print on top left of every page) **1**

    b) **2** (Print on top center of every page) . . **2**

    c) **3** (Print on top right of every page) . . . **3**

    d) **4** (Print on top, alternating
       left and right page) **4**

    e) **5** (Print on bottom left of every page) . . **5**

    f) **6** (Print on bottom center of every page) **6**

    g) **7** (Print bottom right of every page) . . . **7**

    h) **8** (Print on bottom, alternating
       left and right page) **8**

    i) **N** (No page numbers) . . . . **N**

7. Press **F7** (return to document) **F7**

NEW PAGE NUMBER

1. Place cursor at top of page to be renumbered.

2. Press **Shift + F8** (Format) .... `Shift`+`F8`

OR	Pull-down Menu	OR
A) Press **Alt + =**		`Alt`+`=`
B) Select **L** (Layout)		`L`

3. Select **P** (Page) .... `P`

4. Select **N** (Page Numbering) .... `N`

5. Select **N** (New Page Number) .... `N`

6. Type new page number .... Number

7. **Enter** .... `↵`

8. Press **F7** (return to document) .... `F7`

CONDITIONAL END OF PAGE
To protect a certain number of lines from being split by a page break.

1. Place cursor on line above text to be kept together.

2. Press **Shift + F8** (Format) .... `Shift`+`F8`

OR	Pull-down Menu	OR
A) Press **Alt + =**		`Alt`+`=`
B) Select **L** (Layout)		`L`

3. Select **O** (Other) .... `O`

4. Select **C** (Conditional End of Page) .... `C`

5. Type number of lines to be kept together .. Number

6. **Enter** .... `↵`

7. Press **F7** (return to document) .... `F7`

68
HARD PAGE BREAK

INSERT

1. Place cursor where new page is to begin.

2 Press **Ctrl + Enter** . . . . `Ctrl` + `⏎`
   NOTE: A Hard Page break is displayed as a line of equal signs (=).

OR	Pull-down Menu	OR
A) Press **Alt + =**		`Alt` + `=`
B) Select **L** (Layout)		`L`
C) Select **A** (Align)		`A`
D) Select **P** (Hard **P**age)		`P`

DELETE

1. Place cursor immediately after the Hard Page break line.

2. Press **Backspace** (delete Hard Page break). `BkSp`

BLOCK PROTECT

1. Place cursor on first character of text to be protected from a soft page break.

2. Press **Alt + F4** (Block) . . . . `Alt` + `F4`

3. Highlight text (See Block Text on page 10).

4. Press **Shift + F8** (Format) . . . . `Shift` + `F8`
   NOTE: "Protect block?(Y/N)" message appears at bottom left corner of screen.

5. Type **Y** (protect highlighted text) . . . . `Y`

- OR -

Continued ...

Block Protect (continued)

OR	Pull-down Menu	OR
1. Place cursor on first character of text to be protected from a soft page break.		
2. Press **Alt + =**	....	Alt + =
3. Select **E** (Edit)	....	E
4. Select **B** (Block)	....	B
5. Highlight text (see Block Text on page 10).		
6. Press **Alt + =**	....	Alt + =
7. Select **E** (Edit)	....	E
8. Select **T** (Protect Block)	....	T

WIDOW/ORPHAN PROTECTION ON/OFF

1. Place cursor at beginning of document.

2. Press **Shift + F8** (Format) .... Shift + F8

OR	Pull-down Menu	OR
A) Press **Alt + =**	....	Alt + =
B) Select **L** (Layout)	....	L

3. Select **L** (Line) L

4. Select **W** (Widow/Orphan Protection) .... W

5. Type **Y** (on) .... Y

   OR   OR

   Type **N** (off) .... N

6. Press **F7** (return to document) F7

70

HARD SPACE

Will prevent words from breaking during wraparound or pagination (page breaks).

1. Type first word.
2. Press **Home, Spacebar**
   (Hard Space) . . . . |Home| |Space|
3. Type next word.

HYPHENATION

TURNING HYPHENATION ON

1. Place cursor on line where hyphenation change is to begin.
2. Press **Shift + F8** (Format) . . . . |Shift| + |F8|

OR	Pull-down Menu	OR
A) Press **Alt + =**	|Alt| + |=|
B) Select **L** (Layout)	|L|

3. Select **L** (Line) . . . . |L|
4. Select **Y** (Hyphenation) . . . . |Y|
5. Type **Y** (Hyphenation On) . . . . |Y|
6. Press **F7** (return to document) . . . . |F7|
   NOTE: When a word needs to be hyphenated, a beep will sound and the message "Position hyphen; Press ESC" will appear at bottom of screen.
7. Press **Left** or **Right Arrow** . . . . |←| or |→|
8. Press **Esc** (hyphenate word) . . . . |Esc|

Hyphenation (continued)

TURNING HYPHENATION OFF
1. Place cursor on line where hyphenation is to end.
2. Press **Shift + F8** (Format) .... `Shift`+`F8`

OR	Pull-down Menu	OR
A) Press **Alt + =**		`Alt`+`=`
B) Select **L** (Layout)		`L`

3. Select **L** (Line) .... `L`
4. Select **Y** (Hyphenation) .... `Y`
5. Type **N** (Hyphenation Off) .... `N`
6. Press **F7** (return to document) .... `F7`

SETTING H-ZONE
1. Press **Shift + F8** (Format) .... `Shift`+`F8`

OR	Pull-down Menu	OR
A) Press **Alt + =**		`Alt`+`=`
B) Select **L** (Layout)		`L`

2. Select **L** (Line) .... `L`
3. Select **Z** (Set the H-Zone) .... `Z`
4. Type left zone percentage. .... Number
5. **Enter** .... `⏎`
6. Type right zone percentage. .... Number
7. **Enter** .... `⏎`
8. Press **F7** (return to document) .... `F7`

72

CASE CONVERSION
Change an existing block of text to upper or lower case.

1. Place cursor on first character of text to be converted.

2. Press **Alt + F4** (Block) . . . . `Alt`+`F4`

OR	Pull-down Menu	OR
A) Press **Alt + =**		`Alt`+`=`
B) Select **E** (Edit)		`E`
C) Select **B** (Block)		`B`

3. Highlight text (See Block Text on page 10).

4. Press **Shift + F3** (Case Conversion) `Shift`+`F3`

OR	Pull-down Menu	OR
A) Press **Alt + =**		`Alt`+`=`
B) Select **E** (Edit)		`E`
C) Select **V** (Convert Case)		`V`

5. Select **U** (Uppercase) . . . . `U`

OR   OR

Select **L** (Lowercase) . . . . `L`

CAPITALIZATION

1. Press **Caps-Lock** (UPPER CASE). . . . . `Caps Lock`
   NOTE: "Pos" changes to "POS" on the status line.
2. Type text to be in UPPER CASE.

3. Press **Caps-Lock** (End UPPER CASE). . . . . . `Caps Lock`
   NOTE: "POS" changes back to "Pos" on the status line.

COLUMNS

CREATE

1. Press **Alt + F7** (Columns/Table/Math). . $\boxed{Alt}+\boxed{F7}$

OR	**Pull-down Menu**	OR
A) Press **Alt + =**		$\boxed{Alt}+\boxed{=}$
B) Select **L** (Layout)		$\boxed{L}$

2. Select **C** (Columns) . . . . $\boxed{C}$

3. Select **D** (Define) . . . . $\boxed{D}$

4. Select **T** (Type) . . . . $\boxed{T}$

5. Select **one** of the following: Option

   a) **N** (Newspaper) . . . . $\boxed{N}$

   b) **P** (Parallel) . . . . $\boxed{P}$

   c) **B** (Parallel with Block Protect) . . . . $\boxed{B}$

6. Select **N** (Number of Columns) . . . . $\boxed{N}$

7. Type number of columns . . . . Number

8. **Enter** . . . . $\boxed{↵}$
NOTE: Maximum of 24 columns

Create Unequal Columns (Option)

   a) Select **M** (Margins) . . . . $\boxed{M}$

   b) Type Left Margin. . . . . Number

   c) **Enter** . . . . $\boxed{↵}$

   d) Type Right Margin. . . . . Number

   e) **Enter** . . . . $\boxed{↵}$

   f) Repeat steps b-e for each column.

Continued ...

74

Columns (continued)
Create (continued)

Change Distance Between Columns (Option)

   a) Select **D** (Distance Between Columns) . . . . . $\boxed{\text{D}}$

   b) Type Distance Between Columns . . . . . Number

   c) **Enter** . . . . $\boxed{\leftarrow}$

 9. Press **F7** (accept columns setting) . . . . $\boxed{\text{F7}}$

10. Select **O** (On) . . . . $\boxed{\text{O}}$
    NOTE: "Col 1" is added to the status line.
11. Type column text.
    NOTE: Press Ctrl + Enter to move to next column.
12. Repeat step 11 for all columns.

TURN COLUMNS OFF

1. Press **Alt + F7** (Columns/Table/Math). . $\boxed{\text{Alt}}$+$\boxed{\text{F7}}$

OR	**Pull-down Menu**	OR
A) Press **Alt + =**		$\boxed{\text{Alt}}$+$\boxed{=}$
B) Select **L** (Layout)		$\boxed{\text{L}}$

2. Select **C** (Columns) . . . . $\boxed{\text{C}}$

3. Select **F** (Off) . . . . $\boxed{\text{F}}$
    NOTE: "Col" will no longer appears on status line.

Columns (continued)

EDITING COLUMNS

Cursor Movements within a column using Go To (Ctrl + Home)

Select **one** of the following: Option

Previous Column . . . . `Ctrl`+`Home` `←`

Next Column . . . . `Ctrl`+`Home` `→`

First Column . . . `Ctrl`+`Home` `Home` `←`

Last Column . . . `Ctrl`+`Home` `Home` `→`

OR	Pull-down Menu	OR
A) Press **Alt + =**		`Alt`+`=`
B) Select **S** (Search)		`S`
C) Select **G** (Go to)		`G`
D) Select **one** of the following:		Option
Previous Column		`←`
Next Column		`→`
First Column	`Home`	`←`
Last Column	`Home`	`→`

76

MOVE/COPY TEXT WITHIN A COLUMN

1. Place cursor on first character of text to be moved or copied.

2. Press **Alt** + **F4** (Block) . . . .   `Alt`+`F4`

OR	Pull-down Menu	OR
A) Press **Alt** + = ...		`Alt`+`=`
B) Select **E** (Edit)		`E`
C) Select **B** (Block)		`B`

3 Highlight text (see Block Text on page 10).

4. Press **Ctrl** + **F4**, **B** (Move Block). `Ctrl`+`F4` `B`

OR	Pull-down Menu	OR
A) Press **Alt** + = ...		`Alt`+`=`
B) Select **E** (Edit)		`E`

5. Select **M** (Move) . . . . `M`

   OR   **OR**

   Select **C** (Copy) . . . . `C`

6. Place cursor where text is to be moved or copied.

7. **Enter**   . . . . `⏎`

77

Columns (continued)

COLUMN DISPLAY ON/OFF
Displays each column on a separate page instead of side by side.

1. Retrieve document which contains columns.

2. Press **Shift + F1** (Setup) .... **Shift** + **F1**

OR	Pull-down Menu	OR
A) Press **Alt + =**		**Alt** + **=**
B) Select **F** (File)		**F**
C) Select **T** (Setup)		**T**

3. Select **D** (Display) .... **D**

4. Select **E** (Edit-Screen Options) .... **E**

5. Select **S** (Side-by-side Columns Display) ... . **S**

6. Type **Y** (on) .... **Y**

   OR   OR

   Type **N** (off) .... **N**

7. Press **F7** (return to document) **F7**
   NOTE: Columns within every document will be affected by change.

78
HEADERS/FOOTERS

CREATE

NOTE: There can be up to two headers and two footers in a document.

1. Place cursor at top of page where header or footer is to begin.
2. Press **Shift + F8** (Format) . . . . `Shift` + `F8`

OR	Pull-down Menu	OR
A) Press **Alt + =**		`Alt` + `=`
B) Select **L** (Layout)		`L`

3. Select **P** (Page) . . . . `P`
4. Select **H** (Headers) . . . . `H`

   OR   **OR**

   Select **F** (Footers) . . . . `F`

5. Select header type:

   a) **A** (Header A) . . . . `A`

   OR   **OR**

   b) **B** (Header B) . . . . `B`

   OR   **OR**

   Select footer type:

   a) **A** (Footer A) . . . . `A`

   OR   **OR**

   b) **B** (Footer B) . . . . `B`

Continued ...

Headers/Footers (continued)
Create (continued)

6. Select **one** of the following: Option

   a) **P** (Every **P**age) .... 🅿️

   b) **O** (**O**dd Pages) .... 🆂

   c) **V** (E**v**en Pages) .... 🆅

7. Type header or footer text.

8. Press **F7** (save text and return to format menu). F7

9. Press **F7** (return to document) F7

   *NOTE: Headers and footers are not visible on
   screen. Press Alt + F3 (Reveal Codes) to
   view the first 50 characters of text.*

80

EDIT

> *NOTE: WordPerfect searches "backward" through the text to find the header or footer to edit.*

1. Retrieve document which contains header or footer to be edited.

2. Press **Shift + F8** (Format) .... **Shift** + **F8**

OR	Pull-down Menu	OR
A) Press **Alt + =**		**Alt** + **=**
B) Select **L** (Layout)		**L**

3. Select **P** (Page) .... **P**

4. Select **H** (Headers) .... **H**

   OR   **OR**

   Select **F** (Footers) .... **F**

5. Select header type:

   a) **A** (Header A) .... **A**

   OR   **OR**

   b) **B** (Header B) .... **B**

   Select footer type:

   a) **A** (Footer A) .... **A**

   OR   **OR**

   b) **B** (Footer B) .... **B**

5. Select **E** (Edit) .... **E**

6. Edit header or footer.

7. Press **F7** **F7**

8. Press **F7** (return to document) **F7**

FOOTNOTES/ENDNOTES

CREATE

1. Retrieve document which will contain note.

2. Place cursor where footnote or endnote reference number will appear.

3. Press **Ctrl + F7** (Footnote) . . . . `Ctrl`+`F7`

OR	Pull-down Menu	OR
A) Press **Alt + =**		`Alt`+`=`
B) Select **L** (Layout)		`L`

4. Select **F** (Footnote) . . . . `F`

   OR   OR

   Select **E** (Endnote) . . . . `E`

5. Select **C** (Create) . . . . `C`
   NOTE: Reference number will appear on screen.
6. Type footnote or endnote text.

7. Press **F7** (return to document) . . . . `F7`
   NOTE: The reference number will appears in the document on the typing line but will print as a superscript. Footnote text will <u>not</u> appear on screen. Press Alt + F3 (Reveal Codes) to view note.

Footnotes/Endnotes (continued)

EDIT

1. Retrieve document that contains note to be edited.

2. Press **Ctrl + F7** (Footnote) . . . . `Ctrl` + `F7`

OR	Pull-down Menu	OR
A) Press **Alt + =**		`Alt` + `=`
B) Select **L** (Layout)		`L`

3. Select **F** (Footnote) . . . . `F`

   OR   OR

   Select **E** (Endnote) . . . . `E`

4. Select **E** (Edit) . . . . `E`

5. Type number of note to be edited. . . . . Number

6. **Enter** . . . . `↵`

7. Edit note.

8. Press **F7** (return to document) . . . . `F7`

DELETE

1. Retrieve document which contains note to be deleted.

2. Place cursor on note number to be deleted.

3. Press **Delete** . . . . `Del`

4. Type **Y** (confirm deletion) . . . . `Y`
   *NOTE: Remaining reference notations in
   document are automatically renumbered.*

TABLES

CREATE TABLE

1. Place cursor on line where table is to begin.

2. Press Alt + F7 (Columns/Tables/Math). `Alt`+`F7`

OR	Pull-down Menu	OR
A) Press **Alt + =**		`Alt`+`=`
B) Select **L** (Layout)		`L`

3. Select **T** (Tables) .... `T`

4. Select **C** (Create) .... `C`

5. Type number of columns .... Number

6. **Enter** .... `↵`

7. Type number of rows .... Number

8. **Enter** .... `↵`

9. Press **F7** (return to document) .... `F7`

   NOTE: To change the table defaults see Edit
   Table Defaults on pages 85-111.

REMOVE TABLE

1. Place cursor at top left corner of table.

2. Press **Alt + F3** (Reveal codes) .... `Alt`+`F3`

OR	Pull-down Menu	OR
A) Press **Alt + =**		`Alt`+`=`
B) Select **E** (Edit)		`E`
C) Select **R** (Reveal Codes)		`R`

3. Place cursor on **[Tbl Def:]** code to be deleted.

4. Press **Delete** .... `Del`

84

ADD TEXT TO TABLE

1. Place cursor in table.
   NOTE: Cell message appears in status line.
2. Press **Tab** to place cursor in next cell . . . . `Tab`

   OR   **OR**

   Press **Shift** + **Tab** to place cursor
   in previous cell . . . . `Shift` + `Tab`

3. Type or edit text in current cell.
   *NOTE: Cells in the current row will expand as
   you type additional lines of text.*

EDIT TABLE DEFAULTS

EDIT TABLE COLUMN WIDTH
(Using Ctrl + Arrow)

1. Place cursor in table.

2. Press **Alt + F7** (Columns/Tables/Math). `Alt`+`F7`

OR	Pull-down Menu	OR
A) Press **Alt + =**		`Alt`+`=`
B) Select **L** (Layout)		`L`
C) Select **T** (Tables)		`T`
D) Select **E** (Edit)		`E`

3. Place cursor in desired column.

4. Press **Ctrl + Right Arrow**
   (increase size of column until
   desired width) . . . . `Ctrl`+`→`

   OR   OR

   Press **Ctrl + Left Arrow**
   (decrease size of column until
   desired width) . . . . `Ctrl`+`←`

5. Press **F7** (return to document) . . . . `F7`

86

Edit Table Defaults (continued)

EDIT TABLE COLUMN WIDTH

1. Place cursor in table.

2. Press **Alt + F7** (Columns/Tables/Math). `Alt`+`F7`

OR	Pull-down Menu	OR
A) Press **Alt + =**		`Alt`+`=`
B) Select **L** (Layout)		`L`
C) Select **T** (Tables)		`T`
D) Select **E** (Edit)		`E`

3. Place cursor in desired cell.

BLOCK CELLS OPTION (Format Multiple Cells)

a) Press **Alt + F4** (Block) .... `Alt`+`F4`

b) Move cursor to highlight desired cells.

4. Select **F** (Format) .... `F`

5. Select **L** (Column) .... `L`

6. Select **W** (Width) .... `W`

7. Type width of column(s) .... Number

8. **Enter** .... `↵`

9. Press **F7** (return to document) .... `F7`

Edit Table Defaults (continued)

CHANGE TABLE SIZE

1. Place cursor in table.

2. Press **Alt + F7** (Columns/Tables/Math). `Alt`+`F7`

OR	Pull-down Menu	OR
A) Press **Alt + =**		`Alt`+`=`
B) Select **L** (Layout)		`L`
C) Select **T** (Tables)		`T`
D) Select **E** (Edit)		`E`

3. Place cursor in column to be sized.

4. Select **S** (Size) .... `S`

5. Select **R** (Rows) .... `R`

   OR   OR

   Select **C** (Columns) .... `C`

6. Type number of rows or columns .... Number

7. **Enter** .... `⏎`

8. Press **F7** (return to document) .... `F7`

INSERT ROW IN TABLE

1. Place cursor where new row is to be inserted.

2. Press **Ctrl + Insert** (insert new row) .. `Ctrl`+`Ins`

88

Edit Table Defaults (continued)

FORMAT TEXT SIZE IN CELL(S) OR COLUMN

1. Place cursor in table.

2. Press **Alt + F7** (Columns/Tables/Math). $\boxed{\text{Alt}} + \boxed{\text{F7}}$

OR	Pull-down Menu	OR
A) Press **Alt + =**		$\boxed{\text{Alt}} + \boxed{=}$
B) Select **L** (Layout)		$\boxed{\text{L}}$
C) Select **T** (Tables)		$\boxed{\text{T}}$
D) Select **E** (Edit)		$\boxed{\text{E}}$

3. Place cursor in desired cell.

BLOCK CELLS OPTION (Format Multiple Cells)

   a) Press **Alt + F4** (Block) . . . . $\boxed{\text{Alt}} + \boxed{\text{F4}}$

   b) Move cursor to highlight desired cells.

4. Select **F** (Format) . . . . $\boxed{\text{F}}$

5. Select **C** (Cell) . . . . $\boxed{\text{C}}$

   OR   OR

   Select **L** (Column) . . . . $\boxed{\text{L}}$

6. Select **A** (Attributes) . . . . $\boxed{\text{A}}$

7. Select **S** (Size) . . . . $\boxed{\text{S}}$

Continued ...

Edit Table Defaults (continued)
Format Text Size in Cell(s) or Column (continued)

8. Select **one** of the following: **Option**

   a) **P** (Superscript) .... `P`

   b) **B** (Subscript) . ... `B`

   c) **F** (Fine) .... `F`

   d) **S** (Small) .... `S`

   e) **L** (Large) .... `L`

   f) **V** (Very large) .... `V`

   g) **E** (Extra large) .... `E`

9. Press **F7** (return to document) .... `F7`
   NOTE: Each row will automatically adjust to the size of largest font within any column.

FORMAT TEXT APPEARANCE IN CELL(S) OR COLUMN
   NOTE: Each row will automatically adjust to the size of largest font within any column.
1. Place cursor in table.

2. Press **Alt + F7** (Columns/Tables/Math). `Alt`+`F7`

OR	Pull-down Menu	OR
A) Press **Alt + =**		`Alt`+`=`
B) Select **L** (Layout)		`L`
C) Select **T** (Tables)		`T`
D) Select **E** (Edit)		`E`

3. Place cursor in desired cell.

Continued ...

90

Edit Table Defaults (continued)
Format Text Appearance in Cell(s) or Column (continued)

BLOCK CELLS OPTION (Format Multiple Cells)

   a) Press **Alt + F4** (Block) . . . . `Alt`+`F4`

   b) Move cursor to highlight desired cells.

4. Select **F** (Format) . . . . `F`

5. Select **C** (Cell) . . . . `C`

  OR   **OR**

  Select **L** (Column) . . . . `L`

6. Select **A** (Attributes) . . . . `A`

7. Select **A** (Appearance) . . . . `A`

8. Select **one** of the following: **Option**

   a) **B** (Bold) . . . . `B`

   b) **U** (Underline) . . . . `U`

   c) **D** (Dbl Und) . . . . `D`

   d) **I** (Italic) . . . . `I`

   e) **O** (Outline) . . . . `O`

   f) **A** (Shadow) . . . . `A`

   g) **C** (Sm Cap) . . . . `C`

   h) **R** (Redln) . . . . `R`

   i) **S** (Sktout) . . . . `S`

9. Press **F7** (return to document) . . . . `F7`

Edit Table Defaults (continued)

TEXT ATTRIBUTES (RESET OR NORMAL) IN CELL(S) OR COLUMN

NOTE: "Normal" turns off all attributes for the cell. "Reset" returns the cell attributes to the attributes set for the column.

1. Place cursor in table.

2. Press **Alt + F7** (Columns/Tables/Math). `Alt`+`F7`

OR	Pull-down Menu	OR
A) Press **Alt + =**		`Alt`+`=`
B) Select **L** (Layout)		`L`
C) Select **T** (Tables)		`T`
D) Select **E** (Edit)		`E`

3. Place cursor in desired cell.

BLOCK CELLS OPTION (Format Multiple Cells)

   a) Press **Alt + F4** (Block) .... `Alt`+`F4`

   b) Move cursor to highlight desired cells.

4. Select **F** (Format) .... `F`

5. Select **C** (Cell) .... `C`

   OR   OR

   Select **L** (Column) .... `L`

6. Select **A** (Attributes) .... `A`

7. Select **N** (Normal) .... `N`

   OR   OR

   Select **R** (Reset) .... `R`

8. Press **F7** (return to document) .... `F7`

Edit Table Defaults (continued)

JUSTIFY TEXT IN CELL(S) OR COLUMN

NOTE: Justified cells or columns automatically align text within table.

1. Place cursor in table.

2. Press **Alt + F7** (Columns/Tables/Math). `Alt`+`F7`

OR	Pull-down Menu	OR
A) Press **Alt + =**		`Alt`+`=`
B) Select **L** (Layout)		`L`
C) Select **T** (Tables)		`T`
D) Select **E** (Edit)		`E`

3. Place cursor in desired cell.

BLOCK CELLS OPTION (Format Multiple Cells)

a) Press **Alt + F4** (Block) .... `Alt`+`F4`

b) Move cursor to highlight desired cells.

4. Select **F** (Format) .... `F`

5. Select **C** (Cell) .... `C`

   OR   OR

   Select **L** (Column) .... `L`

6. Select **J** (Justify) .... `J`

Continued ...

Edit Table Defaults (continued)
Justify Text in Cell(s) or Columns (continued)

7. Select **one** of the following: **Option**

   a) **L** (Left) . . . . `L`

   b) **C** (Center) . . . . `C`

   c) **R** (Right) . . . . `R`

   d) **F** (Full) . . . . `F`

   e) **D** (Decimal) . . . . `D`

   f) **S** (Reset) . . . . `S`

8. Press **F7** (return to document) . . . . `F7`

FORMAT VERTICAL ALIGNMENT OF CELL

1. Place cursor in table.

2. Press **Alt + F7** (Columns/Tables/Math) . `Alt`+`F7`

OR	Pull-down Menu	OR
A) Press **Alt + =**		`Alt`+`=`
B) Select **L** (Layout)		`L`
C) Select **T** (Tables)		`T`
D) Select **E** (Edit)		`E`

3. Place cursor in desired cell.

4. Select **F** (Format) . . . . `F`

5. Select **C** (Cell) . . . . `C`

6. Select **V** (Vertical Alignment) . . . . `V`

Continued ...

Edit Table Defaults (continued)
Format Vertical Alignment of Cell (continued)

7. Select **one** of the following: **Option**

   a) **T** (Top) . . . .   **T**

   b) **B** (Bottom) . . . .   **B**

   c) **C** (Center) . . . .   **C**

8. Press **F7** (return to document) **F7**

FORMAT TABLE ROW HEIGHT

1. Place cursor in table.

2. Press **Alt + F7** (Columns/Tables/Math).   **Alt**+**F7**

OR	**Pull-down Menu**	OR
A) Press **Alt + =**		**Alt**+**=**
B) Select **L** (Layout)		**L**
C) Select **T** (Tables)		**T**
D) Select **E** (Edit)		**E**

3. Place cursor in desired cell.

BLOCK CELLS OPTION (Format Multiple Cells)

   a) Press **Alt + F4** (Block) . . . .   **Alt**+**F4**

   b) Move cursor to highlight desired cells.

4. Select **F** (Format) . . . .   **F**

5. Select **R** (Row Height) . . . .   **R**

Continued ...

Edit Table Defaults (continued)
Format Table Row Height (continued)

6. Select **one** of the following: **Option**

   a) **F** (Fixed, Single line) . . . . ⬛ F

      1) Type height (decimal number) . . . Number

      2) **Enter** . . . . ⬛↵

   b) **T** (Auto, Single line) . . . . ⬛ T

   c) **X** (Fixed Multi-line) . . . . ⬛ X

      1) Type height (decimal number) . . . Number

      2) **Enter** . . . . ⬛↵

   d) **A** (Auto, Multi-line) . . . . ⬛ A

7. Press **F7** (return to document) . . . . ⬛ F7

CHANGE TABLE LINE TYPE

1. Place cursor in table.

2. Press **Alt + F7** (Columns/Tables/Math) . ⬛ Alt + ⬛ F7

OR	Pull-down Menu	OR
A) Press **Alt + =**		⬛ Alt + ⬛ =
B) Select **L** (Layout)		⬛ L
C) Select **T** (Tables)		⬛ T
D) Select **E** (Edit)		⬛ E

3. Place cursor in desired cell.

Continued ...

96

Edit Table Defaults (continued)
Change Table Line Type (continued)

BLOCK CELLS OPTION (Format Multiple Cells)

  a) Press **Alt + F4** (Block) . . . . `Alt` + `F4`

  b) Move cursor to highlight desired cells.

4. Select **L** (Lines) . . . . `L`

5. Select **one** of the following: Option

  a) **L** (Left) . . . . `L`

  b) **R** (Right) . . . . `R`

  c) **T** (Top) . . . . `T`

  d) **B** (Bottom) . . . . `B`

  e) **I** (Inside) . . . . `I`

  f) **O** (Outside) . . . . `O`

  g) **A** (All, if blocked) . . . . `A`

  h) **S** (Shade, text area) . . . . `S`

6. Select **one** of the following: Option

  a) **N** (None) . . . . `N`

  b) **S** (Single) . . . . `S`

  c) **D** (Double) . . . . `D`

  d) **A** (Dashed) . . . . `A`

  e) **O** (Dotted) . . . . `O`

  f) **T** (Thick) . . . . `T`

  g) **E** (Extra thick) . . . . `E`

7. Press **F7** (return to document) . . . . `F7`

Edit Table Defaults (continued)

EDIT ALL LINES IN A TABLE

1. Place cursor in table.

2. Press **Alt + F7** (Columns/Tables/Math). `Alt`+`F7`

OR	Pull-down Menu	OR
A) Press **Alt + =**		`Alt`+`=`
B) Select **L** (Layout)		`L`
C) Select **T** (Tables)		`T`
D) Select **E** (Edit)		`E`

3. Place cursor in cell A1.

4. Press **Alt + F4** (Block) .... `Alt`+`F4`

5. Press **Home, Home, Down.** `Home` `Home` `↓`

6. Select **L** (Lines) .... `L`

7. Select **A** (All) .... `A`

8. Select **one** of the following: Option

   a) **N** (None - to remove all lines) .... `N`

   b) **S** (Single) .... `S`

   c) **D** (Double) .... `D`

   d) **A** (Dashed) .... `A`

   e) **O** (Dotted) .... `O`

   f) **T** (Thick) .... `T`

   g) **E** (Extra thick) .... `E`

9. Press **F7** (return to document) .... `F7`

98

Edit Table Defaults (continued)

CREATE A TABLE HEADER

> *Note: Table headers are used for a table that spans*
> *more than one page. Text typed in rows that*
> *are designated as header rows will repeat*
> *within the same rows on subsequent pages.*
> *Typed text in header rows will not appear on*
> *next pages but will be printed. See View*
> *Document on Screen on page 95.*

1. Place cursor in table.

2. Press **Alt + F7** (Columns/Tables/Math) . `Alt`+`F7`

OR	Pull-down Menu	OR
A) Press **Alt + =**		`Alt`+`=`
B) Select **L** (Layout)		`L`
C) Select **T** (Tables)		`T`
D) Select **E** (Edit)		`E`

3. Select **H** (Header) .... `H`

4. Type number of Header rows .... Number

5. **Enter** .... `⏎`

6. Press **F7** (return to document) .... `F7`

Edit Table Defaults (continued)

SPACING BETWEEN TEXT AND TABLE LINES
*NOTE: Spacing between text and lines allows you
        to specify the amount of white space
        between text in each cell and the lines
        that make up the cell.*
1. Place cursor in table.

2. Press **Alt + F7** (Columns/Tables/Math) . `Alt`+`F7`

OR	Pull-down Menu	OR
A) Press **Alt + =**		`Alt`+`=`
B) Select **L** (Layout)		`L`
C) Select **T** (Tables)		`T`
D) Select **E** (Edit)		`E`

3. Select **O** (Options) .... `O`
4. Select **S** (Spacing Between Text and Lines) ... `S`

   a) Type number for left spacing .... Number

   b) **Enter** .... `↵`

   c) Type number for right spacing .... Number

   d) **Enter** .... `↵`

   e) Type number for top spacing .... Number

   f) **Enter** .... `↵`

   g) Type number for bottom spacing ...... Number

   h) **Enter** .... `↵`

5. Press **F7** (return to table edit) .... `F7`
6. Press **F7** (return to document) .... `F7`

CHANGE POSITION OF TABLE

1. Place cursor in table.

2. Press **Alt + F7** (Columns/Tables/Math) . `Alt`+`F7`

OR	Pull-down Menu	OR
A) Press **Alt + =**		`Alt`+`=`
B) Select **L** (Layout)		`L`
C) Select **T** (Tables)		`T`
D) Select **E** (Edit)		`E`

3. Select **O** (Options) . . . . `O`

4. Select **P** (Position of table) . . . . `P`

5. Select **one** of the following: **Option**

   a) **L** (Left) . . . . `L`

   b) **R** (Right) . . . . `R`

   c) **C** (Center) . . . . `C`

   d) **F** (Full) . . . . `F`

   e) **S** (Set position) . . . . `S`

      1) Type number (offset from left edge). Number

      2) **Enter** . . . . `↵`

6. **Enter** . . . . `↵`

7. Press **F7** (return to table edit) . . . . `F7`

8. Press **F7** (return to document) . . . . `F7`

Edit Table Defaults (continued)

GRAY SHADING OF TABLE

1. Place cursor in table.

2. Press **Alt + F7** (Columns/Tables/Math) . `Alt`+`F7`

OR	Pull-down Menu	OR
A) Press **Alt + =**		`Alt`+`=`
B) Select **L** (Layout)		`L`
C) Select **T** (Tables)		`T`
D) Select **E** (Edit)		`E`

3. Select **O** (Options) .... `O`

4. Select **G** (Grey shading (% of black) .... `G`

5. Type number (percent of black) .... Number

6. **Enter** .... `↵`

7. Press **F7** (return to table edit) .... `F7`

8. Press **F7** (return to document) .... `F7`

JOIN CELLS OF A TABLE

1. Place cursor in table.

2. Press **Alt + F7** (Columns/Tables/Math) . `Alt`+`F7`

OR	Pull-down Menu	OR
A) Press **Alt + =**		`Alt`+`=`
B) Select **L** (Layout)		`L`
C) Select **T** (Tables)		`T`
D) Select **E** (Edit)		`E`

Continued ...

Edit Table Defaults (continued)
Join Cells of a Table (continued)

3. Place cursor in first cell to be joined.

4. Press **Alt + F4** (Block) . . . . `Alt`+`F4`

5. Move cursor to highlight cells to be joined.

6. Select **J** (Join) . . . . `J`

7. Type **Y** (Yes) . . . . `Y`

8. Press **F7** (return to document) . . . . `F7`

SPLIT CELLS OF A TABLE

1. Place cursor in table.

2. Press **Alt + F7** (Columns/Tables/Math). `Alt`+`F7`

OR	Pull-down Menu	OR
A) Press **Alt + =**		`Alt`+`=`
B) Select **L** (Layout)		`L`
C) Select **T** (Tables)		`T`
D) Select **E** (Edit)		`E`

3. Place cursor in desired cell.

BLOCK CELLS OPTION (Format Multiple Cells)

a) Press **Alt + F4** (Block) . . . . `Alt`+`F4`

b) Move cursor to highlight desired cells.

4. Select **P** (Split) . . . . `P`

Continued ...

Edit Table Defaults (continued)
Split Cells of a Table (continued)

5. Select **R** (Rows) .... R

   OR   OR

   Select **C** (Columns) C

6. Type number (of columns or rows) .... Number

7. **Enter** .... ↵

8. Press **F7** (return to document) F7

CREATE A MATH TABLE

1. Place cursor on line where table is to be placed.

2. Press **Alt + F7** (Columns/Tables/Math). Alt + F7

  OR   **Pull-down Menu**   OR

  A) Press **Alt + =** .... Alt + =

  B) Select **L** (Layout) L

  C) Select **T** (Tables) .... T

  D) Select **C** (Create) C

3. Type number of columns .... Number

4. **Enter** .... ↵

5. Type number of rows .... Number

6. **Enter** .... ↵

7. Place cursor in desired cell.

8. Select **M** (Math) .... M

9. Select **F** (Formula) .... F

Continued ...

104

Edit Table Defaults (continued)
Create a Math Table (continued)

10. Type desired formula when prompted.
    Example: (B2+C2+C3)/3

11. **Enter** . . . . ⏎

12. Repeat steps 10 and 11 to define other cells.

13. Press **F7** (return to document) F7

FUNCTIONS IN MATH TABLES

1. Place cursor in table.

2. Press **Alt + F7** (Columns/Tables/Math) . Alt + F7

OR	**Pull-down Menu**	OR
A) Press **Alt + =**		Alt + =
B) Select **L** (Layout)		L
C) Select **T** (Tables)		T
D) Select **E** (Edit)		E

3. Place cursor in desired cell.

4. Select **M** (Math) . . . . M

5. Select **one** of the following: **Option**

   a) **+** (Subtotal) . . . . +
      adds numbers directly above the function

   b) **=** (Total) . . . . =
      adds subtotals directly above the function

   c) ***** (Grand total) . . . . *
      adds totals directly above the function

   *NOTE: Results are calculated when you Select
          Math Calculate option*

6. Repeat steps 3-5 to define functions for other cells.

7. Press **F7** (return to document) F7

Edit Table Defaults (continued)

COPY FORMULA IN MATH TABLE

1. Place cursor in table.

2. Press **Alt + F7** (Columns/Tables/Math) . `Alt`+`F7`

OR	Pull-down Menu	OR
A) Press **Alt + =**		`Alt`+`=`
B) Select **L** (Layout)		`L`
C) Select **T** (Tables)		`T`
D) Select **E** (Edit)		`E`

3. Place cursor in cell that contains formula.

4. Select **M** (Math) . . . . `M`

5. Select **P** (Copy Formula) . . . . `P`

6. Select **one** of the following: Option

   a) **C** (Cell) . . . . `C`

     1) Move cursor to target cell.

     2) **Enter** . . . . `↵`

   b) **D** (Down) . . . . `D`

     1) Type number of times to copy . . . Number

     2) **Enter** . . . . `↵`

   c) **R** (Right) . . . . `R`

     1) Type number of times to copy . . . Number

     2) **Enter** . . . . `↵`

7. Press **F7** (return to document) . . . . `F7`

Edit Table Defaults (continued)

FORMAT DISPLAY OF NEGATIVE RESULTS IN TABLE CALCULATIONS

1. Place cursor in table.

2. Press **Alt + F7** (Columns/Tables/Math). **Alt** + **F7**

OR	Pull-down Menu	OR
A) Press **Alt + =**		**Alt** + **=**
B) Select **L** (Layout)		**L**
C) Select **T** (Tables)		**T**
D) Select **E** (Edit)		**E**

3. Select **O** (Options) .... **O**

4. Select **D** (Display negative results) .... **D**

5. Select **1** (with minus sign) **1**

   OR   OR

   Select **2** (with parenthesis) **2**

6. **Enter** .... **⏎**

7. Press **F7** (return to document) **F7**

Edit Table Defaults (continued)

LOCK OR UNLOCK TABLE CELL(S)

1. Place cursor in table.

2. Press **Alt + F7** (Columns/Tables/Math). `Alt`+`F7`

OR	**Pull-down Menu**	OR
A) Press **Alt + =**		`Alt`+`=`
B) Select **L** (Layout)		`L`
C) Select **T** (Tables)		`T`
D) Select **E** (Edit)		`E`

3. Place cursor in desired cell.

BLOCK CELLS OPTION (Format Multiple Cells)

   a) Press **Alt + F4** (Block) . . . . `Alt`+`F4`

   b) Move cursor to highlight desired cells.

4. Select **F** (Format) . . . . `F`

5. Select **C** (Cell) . . . . `C`

6. Select **L** (Lock) . . . . `L`

7. Select **O** (On) . . . . `O`

   OR   **OR**

   Select **F** (Off) . . . . `F`

8. Press **F7** (return to document) . . . . `F7`

   NOTE: Text in locked cells cannot be assessed without changing the lock condition to off.

Edit Table Defaults (continued)

REMOVE FORMULA IN MATH TABLE

1. Place cursor in table.

2. Press **Alt + F7** (Columns/Tables/Math) . `Alt`+`F7`

OR	Pull-down Menu	OR
A) Press **Alt + =**		`Alt`+`=`
B) Select **L** (Layout)		`L`
C) Select **T** (Tables)		`T`
D) Select **E** (Edit)		`E`

3. Place cursor in cell that contains formula.

4. Select **F** (Format) .... `F`

5. Select **C** (Cell) .... `C`

6. Select **T** (Type) .... `T`

7. Select **T** (Text) .... `T`

   *NOTE: Formulas and results remain on the
   screen until removed through editing cell
   contents.*

8. Press **F7** (return to document) .... `F7`

9. Place cursor in cell that contains formula.

10. Press **Delete** to remove result of formula .... `Del`

Edit Table Defaults (continued)

CALCULATIONS WITHIN A TABLE

> *NOTE: This procedure requires math formulas within an existing table. See Create Math Table on pages 103 and 104.*

1. Place cursor in table.

2. Press **Tab** to place cursor in desired cell .... `Tab`

3. Type number to be calculated .... Number

4. Repeat steps 2 and 3 for each cell to be calculated.

5. Press **Alt + F7** (Columns/Tables/Math) . `Alt`+`F7`

OR	Pull-down Menu	OR
A) Press **Alt + =**		`Alt`+`=`
B) Select **L** (Layout)		`L`
C) Select **T** (Tables)		`T`
D) Select **E** (Edit)		`E`

6. Select **M** (Math) .... `M`

7. Select **C** (Calculate) .... `C`

8. Press **F7** (return to document) .... `F7`

110

Edit Table Defaults (continued)

FORMAT CELL TYPE DEFINITION
NOTE: Cells are numeric by default.
1. Place cursor in table.

2. Press **Alt + F7** (Columns/Tables/Math). `Alt`+`F7`

OR	**Pull-down Menu**	OR
A) Press **Alt + =**		`Alt`+`=`
B) Select **L** (Layout)		`L`
C) Select **T** (Tables)		`T`
D) Select **E** (Edit)		`E`

3. Place cursor in desired cell.

4. Press **F** (Format) .... `F`

5. Select **C** (Cell) .... `C`

6. Select **T** (Type) .... `T`

7. Select **N** (Numeric) .... `N`

   OR   **OR**

   Select **T** (Text) .... `T`

8. Press **F7** (return to document) .... `F7`

Edit Table Defaults (continued)

FORMAT DIGIT LIMIT OF CELL

1. Place cursor in table.

2. Press **Alt + F7** (Columns/Tables/Math) . `Alt`+`F7`

OR	Pull-down Menu	OR
A) Press **Alt + =**		`Alt`+`=`
B) Select **L** (Layout)		`L`
C) Select **T** (Tables)		`T`
D) Select **E** (Edit)		`E`

3. Place cursor in desired cell.

BLOCK CELLS OPTION (Format Multiple Cells)

  a) Press **Alt + F4** (Block) .... `Alt`+`F4`

  b) Use cursor movement keys to highlight desired cells.

4. Select **F** (Format) .... `F`

5. Select **L** (Column) .... `L`

6. Select **D** (Digits) .... `D`

7. Type number of digits .... Number

8. **Enter** .... `↵`

9. Press **F7** (return to document) .... `F7`

112

MATH

DEFINING COLUMNS

1. Set Tabs (see Tab Set section).

2. Press **Alt + F7** (Columns/Tables/Math) . `Alt`+`F7`

OR	Pull-down Menu	OR
A) Press **Alt + =**		`Alt`+`=`
B) Select **L** (Layout)		`L`

3. Select **M** (Math) .... `M`

4. Select **D** (Define) .... `D`

5. Select **one** of the following: Option

   a) **0** (Calculation) .... `0`

   b) **1** (Text) .... `1`

   c) **2** (Numeric) .... `2`

   d) **3** (Total) .... `3`

For column type **0** (Calculation), type formula.

	Formula	Result
Example:	A+B	Sum of Columns A and B

NOTE: There are four operators used to create a formula:
   + add, - subtract, * multiply, / divide.

6. **Enter** .... `⏎`

7. Repeat step 5 for other columns.

   NOTE: A maximum of four calculation columns
      can be created.

8. **Enter** .... `⏎`

9. Press **F7** .... `F7`

10. Press **F7** (return to document) .... `F7`

Math (continued)

CALCULATIONS WITHIN A DOCUMENT

1. Set Tabs (see Tab Set section).

2. Press **Alt + F7** (Columns/Tables/Math) . **Alt**+**F7**

OR	Pull-down Menu	OR
A) Press **Alt + =**		**Alt**+**=**
B) Select **L** (Layout)		**L**

3. Select **M** (Math) . . . . **M**

   *NOTE: Math message appears at the bottom
   of screen.*

4. Select **O** (On) . . . . **O**

5. Type numbers to be calculated . . . . Number

   a) **Tab** (to column) . . . . **Tab**

   b) Type numbers . . . . Number

   *NOTE: An ! (formula operator) will appear in the
   calculation column. Do not enter
   numbers in a calculation column.*

   c) Repeat steps a and b for each "math" column.

   d) **Enter** (move to next line) . . . .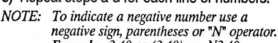

   e) Repeat steps a-d for each line of numbers.

   *NOTE: To indicate a negative number use a
   negative sign, parentheses or "N" operator.
   Example: -3.40 or (3.40) or N3.40.*

Continued ...

114

Math (continued)
Calculations Within a Document (continued)

6. To Calculate:

SUBTOTAL

a) **Enter** (move to next line) . . . .

b) **Tab** (move to column to be calculated) . . . . `Tab`

c) Type **+** (create subtotal) . . . . `+`

d) Repeat steps b and c for all columns to be calculated.

e) Press **Alt + F7** (Columns/Tables/Math) `Alt`+`F7`

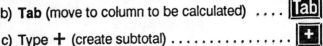

OR	Pull-down Menu	OR
A) Press **Alt + =**		`Alt`+`=`
B) Select **L** (Layout)		`L`

f) Select **M** (Math) . . . . `M`

g) Select **C** (Calculate) . . . . `C`

TOTAL (add subtotals)

a) **Enter** (move to next line) . . . .

b) **Tab** (move to column to be calculated) . . . . `Tab`

c) Type **=** (create total) . . . .

d) Repeat steps b and c for all columns to be calculated.

Continued ...

115

Math (continued)
Calculations Within a Document (continued)
Total (continued)

e) Press **Alt + F7** (Columns/Tables/Math)   `Alt` + `F7`

OR	Pull-down Menu	OR
A) Press **Alt + =**		`Alt` + `=`
B) Select **L** (Layout)		`L`

f) Select **M** (Math) .... `M`

g) Select **C** (Calculate) .... `C`

GRAND TOTAL (Add Totals)

a) **Enter** (move to next line) .... `↵`

b) **Tab** (move to column to be calculated) .... `Tab`

c) Type **T** .... `T`

d) Type number .... Number
   Example: T2000.00

e) Repeat steps b-d for all columns.

f) **Enter** .... `↵`

g) **Enter** (add more spacing) .... `↵`

h) **Tab** (move to column to be calculated) .... `Tab`

i) Type ***** (create grand total) .... `*`

J) Repeat steps h and i for all columns.

Continued ...

116

k) Press **Alt + F7** (Columns/Tables/Math). `Alt`+`F7`

OR	Pull-down Menu	OR
A) Press **Alt + =**		`Alt`+`=`
B) Select **L** (Layout)		`L`

l) Select **M** (Math) . . . . `M`

m) Select **C** (Calculate) . . . . `C`

> *NOTE:* *Type* ***t*** *before number to be calculated as a subtotal. Type* ***T*** *before number to be calculated as a Grand total.*

CALCULATION COLUMN

a) **Tab** (calculate column(s)) . . . . `Tab`

> *NOTE:* *An ! (formula operator) will appear in the calculation column. Do not enter numbers in a calculation column.*

b) Press **Alt + F7** (Columns/Tables/Math). `Alt`+`F7`

OR	Pull-down Menu	OR
A) Press **Alt + =**		`Alt`+`=`
B) Select **L** (Layout)		`L`

c) Select **M** (Math) . . . . `M`

d) Select **C** (Calculate) . . . . `C`

> *NOTE:* *Result of calculation column will be displayed.*

TEXT COLUMN

1. **Tab** (move to text column) . . . . `Tab`

2. Type Text.

Math (continued)

TURN MATH OFF

1. Press **Alt + F7** (Columns/Tables/Math).

OR	Pull-down Menu	OR
A) Press **Alt + =**		$\boxed{Alt}+\boxed{=}$
B) Select **L** (Layout)		$\boxed{L}$

2. Select **M** (Math) .... $\boxed{M}$

3. Select **F** (Off) .... $\boxed{F}$

*NOTE: The Math operators (+, =, T, *, etc.)*
appear on the screen but do not print.

MERGE

CREATE A SECONDARY FILE
OF MERGE RECORDS

NOTE: A <u>Record</u> contains a group of related
fields. A record may contain information
on a particular person or item.
A <u>field</u> is a single element in a record. A
field may contain, for example, a title, first
name or last name.

1. Clear screen (see Clear Screen on page 8).

2. Type data for first merge field.

3. Press **F9** (End Field) .... $\boxed{F9}$

4. Repeat steps 2 and 3 for each field.

NOTE: If a field within a record is blank, Press
F9 (End Field). This marks a position for
that field in the record. There must be the
same number of fields in every record.

5. Press **Shift + F9** (Merge Codes). .... $\boxed{Shift}+\boxed{F9}$

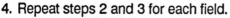

Continued ...

118

Merge (continued)
Create a Secondary File of Merge Records (continued)

6. Select **E** (End Record) .... 🇪
   NOTE: This will also insert a page break.
7. Repeat steps 2-6 for each record.

8. Press **F7** (Save) F7

OR	Pull-down Menu	OR
A) Press **Alt + =**		Alt + ═
B) Select **F** (File)		🇫
C) Select **X** (Exit)		🇽

9. Type **Y** (Save document) .... 🇾

10. Type document name. .... Filename
    *NOTE: Use a .sf extension to identify the
    document as a secondary file.
    Example: LETTER.SF*

11. **Enter** .... ⏎

12. **Enter** .... ⏎

Example:

Without a Blank Field

Mr.{END FIELD}
Anthony{END FIELD}
Salazar{END FIELD}
Marketing Dept{END FIELD}
Tri-Star Music Inc.{END FIELD}
212 Cypress Lane{END FIELD}
Yonkers{END FIELD}
NY{END FIELD}
10312{END FIELD}
{END RECORD}

With a Blank Field

Ms.
{END FIELD}
Rich{END FIELD}
{END FIELD}
DDC{END FIELD}
14 East 38th St.{END FIELD}
New York{END FIELD}
NY{END FIELD}
10016{END FIELD}
{END RECORD}

Merge (continued)

CREATE A PRIMARY FILE

> *NOTE: Each field in a record is numbered*
> *Example: {FIELD}1~ =Title*
> *{FIELD}2~ =First name*

1. Place cursor on line where field is to be placed.

2. Press **Shift + F9** (Merge Codes) ... **Shift** + **F9**

OR	Pull-down Menu	OR
A) Press **Alt + =**		**Alt** + **=**
B) Select **T** (Tools)		**T**
C) Select **R** (Merge)		**R**

3. Select **F** (Field) .... **F**

4. Type field number .... Number

5. **Enter** .... ⏎

6. Repeat steps 1-6 for each field.

7. Type remainder of document.

Continued ...

120

Merge (continued)
Create a Primary File (continued)

8. Press **F7** (Save) . . . . `F7`

OR	**Pull-down Menu**	OR
A) Press **Alt + =**		`Alt`+`=`
B) Select **F** (File)		`F`
C) Select **X** (Exit)		`X`

9. Type **Y** (Save document) . . . . `Y`

10. Type document name . . . . Filename

> *NOTE: Use a .pf extension to identify the document as a primary file.*
> *Example: LETTER.PF*

11. **Enter** . . . . `⏎`

12. **Enter** . . . . `⏎`

Example:

Primary File	Merged Record
{FIELD}1~ {FIELD}2~ {FIELD}3~ {FIELD}4~ {FIELD}5~ {FIELD}6~ {FIELD}7~ {FIELD}8~ {FIELD}9~ Dear {FIELD}1~ {FIELD}3~: Thank you, {FIELD}1~ {FIELD}3~, for...	Mr. Anthony Salazar Marketing Dept Tri-Star Music Inc. 2121 Cypress Lane Yonkers, NY 10312 Dear Mr. Salazar: Thank you, Mr. Salazar, for...

Merge (continued)

ELIMINATE BLANK LINES IN A RECORD WHEN A FIELD REPRESENTS A COMPLETE LINE

1. Press **Shift + F9** (Merge Codes) . . . **Shift** + **F9**

OR	Pull-down Menu	OR
A) Press **Alt + =**		**Alt** + **=**
B) Select **T** (Tools)		**T**
C) Select **R** (Merge)		**R**

2. Select **F** (Field) . . . . **F**

3. Type field number . . . . Number

4. Type a question mark . . . . **?**

5. Enter . . . . **↵**
   Example: {FIELD}4?~

   NOTE: *If a field is blank and represents an entire line, the question mark prevents a blank line form appearing in the merged document.*

Example:

Primary File (with a blank line)	Merged Record
{FIELD}1~ {FIELD}2~ {FIELD}3~ {FIELD}4?~ {FIELD}5~ {FIELD}6~ {FIELD}7~ {FIELD}8~ {FIELD}9~	Ms. Rich Dictation Disc Co. 14 East 38th St New York, NY 10016
Dear {FIELD}1~ {FIELD}3~:	Dear Ms. Rich: Thank you, Ms. Rich, for...
Thank you, {FIELD}1~ {FIELD}3~, for...	

122

CREATE A MERGED DOCUMENT

1. Press **Ctrl + F9** (Merge/Sort) .... `Ctrl` + `F9`

OR	Pull-down Menu	OR
A) Press **Alt + =** .... `Alt` + `=`
B) Select **T** (Tools) .... `T`

2. Select **M** (Merge) .... `M`

3. Type name of primary file. .... Filename

4. **Enter** .... `↵`

5. Type name of secondary file. .... Filename

6. **Enter** .... `↵`

   NOTE: The merged document will appear on screen.

SAVE MERGED DOCUMENT

1. Press **F7** (Exit) .... `F7`

OR	Pull-down Menu	OR
A) Press **Alt + =** .... `Alt` + `=`
B) Select **F** (File) .... `F`
C) Select **X** (Exit) .... `X`

2. Type **Y** (Save document) .... `Y`

3. Type document name .... Filename

4. **Enter** .... `↵`

   NOTE: To print document see Print on pages 19-21.

Merge (continued)

TO CREATE A SECONDARY FILE FOR ENVELOPES
See Create a Secondary File of Merge Records on
pages 117 and 118.

ENVELOPES (Primary File)
*NOTE: This example shows the steps for hand-
feeding envelopes (9" X 4").*

1. Clear screen (see Clear Screen on page 8).

2. Press **Shift + F8** (Format) . . . . `Shift`+`F8`

OR	Pull-down Menu	OR
A) Press **Alt + =**		`Alt`+`=`
B) Select **L** (Layout)		`L`

3. Select **P** (Page) . . . . `P`

4. Select **S** (Size/Type) . . . . `S`

5. Select **A** (Add) . . . . `A`

6. Select **E** (Envelope) . . . . `E`

7. Select **S** (Paper Size) . . . . `S`

8. Select **E** (Envelope) 9.5" x 4" . . . . `E`

9. **Enter** . . . . `↵`

10. Select **S** (Select) . . . . `S`

11. **Enter** . . . . `↵`

12. Select **L** (Line) . . . . `L`

Continued ...

Merge (continued)
Envelopes (Primary File continued)

13. Select **M** (Margins Left/Right) .... `M`

14. Type **4.5** (Left Margin) .... `4` `.` `5`

15. **Enter** .... `↵`

16. Type **0** (Right Margin) .... `0`

17. **Enter** .... `↵`

18. **Enter** .... `↵`

19. Select **P** (Page) .... `P`

20. Select **M** (Margins Top/Bottom) .... `M`

21. Type **0** (Top Margin) .... `0`

22. **Enter** .... `↵`

23. Type **0** (Bottom Margin) .... `0`

24. **Enter** .... `↵`

25. **Enter** .... `↵`

26. Select **O** (Other) .... `O`

27. Select **A** (Advance) .... `A`

28. Select **D** (Down) .... `D`

29. Type **1.5** .... `1` `.` `5`

30. **Enter** .... `↵`

31. Press **F7** (return to document) .... `F7`

32. Repeat steps 1-6 of Create a Primary File on pages 119-121 to place name and address lines.

Continued ...

Merge (continued)
Envelopes (Primary File continued)

Example:
Primary File	Merged Record
{FIELD}1~ {FIELD}2~ {FIELD}3~	Mr. Stuart Auslander
{FIELD}4~	Riverdale Shipping
{FIELD}5~	121 Mariners Drive
{FIELD}6~ {FIELD}7~ {FIELD}8~	Spring, ME 01342

33. Press **F7** (Exit) . . . .

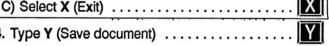

OR	**Pull-down Menu**	**OR**
A) Press **Alt + =**		[Alt]+[=]
B) Select **F** (File)		[F]
C) Select **X** (Exit)		[X]

34. Type **Y** (Save document) . . . . [Y]

35. Type document name . . . . Filename
    Example: ENVELOPE.PF

36. **Enter** . . . . ⏎

37. **Enter** . . . . ⏎

CREATE MERGED DOCUMENT (Envelopes)
See Create a Merged Document on page 122.

PRINT MERGED DOCUMENT (Envelopes)
See Print on pages 19-21.

126

SAVE MERGED DOCUMENT (Envelope)

1. Press **F7** (Exit) .... `F7`

OR	Pull-down Menu	OR
A) Press **Alt + =**		`Alt`+`=`
B) Select **F** (File)		`F`
C) Select **X** (Exit)		`X`

2. Type **Y** (Save document) .... `Y`

3. Type document name. .... Filename

4. **Enter** .... `⏎`

5. **Enter** .... `⏎`

   NOTE: To print document see Print on
   pages 19 - 21.

LABELS (Secondary File)
See Create a Secondary File of Merged Records section.

Example:
Secondary File (one record)
Mr.**{END FIELD}**
Stuart**{END FIELD}**
Auslander**{END FIELD}**
Riverdale Shipping**{END FIELD}**
121 Mariners Drive**{END FIELD}**
Spring, ME 01342 **[END FIELD]**
{END RECORD}

Merge (continued)

LABELS (Primary File)

NOTE: This example shows the steps for 4" X 1 7/16" labels.

1. Clear screen (see Clear Screen on page 8).

2. Press **Shift + F8** (Format) . . . . `Shift` + `F8`

OR	Pull-down Menu	OR
A) Press **Alt + =**		`Alt` + `=`
B) Select **L** (Layout)		`L`

3. Select **D** (Document) . . . . `D`

4. Select **C** (Initial Codes) . . . . `C`

5. Press **Shift + F8** (Format) . . . . `Shift` + `F8`

OR	Pull-down Menu	OR
A) Press **Alt + =**		`Alt` + `=`
B) Select **L** (Layout)		`L`

6. Select **P** (Page) . . . . `P`

7. Select **S** (Paper Size/Type) . . . . `S`

8. Select **A** (Add) . . . . `A`

9. Select **L** (Labels) . . . . `L`

10. Select **S** (Paper Size) . . . . `S`

11. Select **O** (Other) . . . . `O`

12. Type **8.25** (Width of sheet) . . . . . `8` `.` `2` `5`

13. **Enter** . . . . `↵`

14. Type **12.0** (Height of paper) . . . . `1` `2` `.` `0`

15. **Enter** . . . . `↵`

Continued ...

Merge (continued)
Labels (Primary File continued)

16. Select **A** (Labels) .... `A`

17. Type **Y** .... `Y`

18. Select **S** (Size) .... `S`

19. Type **4.0** (Width of individual label) ... `4` `.` `0`

20. **Enter** .... `↵`

21. Type **1.44** (Height of label) ..... `1` `.` `4` `4`

22. **Enter** .... `↵`

23. Select **N** (Number of labels) .... `N`

24. Type **2** (Number of columns) .... `2`

25. **Enter** .... `↵`

26. Type **8** (Number of rows) .... `8`

27. **Enter** .... `↵`

28. Select **D** (Distance between labels) .... `D`

29. Type **.25** (Distance between columns). `.` `2` `5`

30. **Enter** .... `↵`

31. Type **.063** .... `.` `0` `6` `3`
    (Distance between rows)

32. **Enter** .... `↵`

33. Select **C** (Top Left Corner) .... `C`

34. Type **.063** (Distance from top of
    sheet top of first row of labels) .. `.` `0` `6` `3`

35. **Enter** .... `↵`

Continued ...

Merge (continued)
Labels (Primary File continued)

36. Type **0** (Distance from left edge of paper to left edge of first column) . . . . `0`

NOTE: Exclude edge for tractor feed sheets.

37. **Enter** . . . . `⏎`

38. Select **M** (Label Margins) . . . . `M`

39. Type Left Margin . . . . Number

40. **Enter** . . . . `⏎`

41. Type Right Margin . . . . Number

42. **Enter** . . . . `⏎`

43. Type Top Margin . . . . Number

44. **Enter** . . . . `⏎`

45. Type Bottom Margin . . . . Number

46. **Enter** . . . . `⏎`

47. Press **F7** (return to Paper Definition Menu) . . . `F7`

48. Press **F7** (return to Paper Size/Type Menu) . . `F7`

49. Select **S** (Select New Definition) . . . . `S`

50. Press **F7** (return to Initial Codes) . . . . `F7`

51. Press **F7** (return to Format Document menu) . `F7`

52. Press **F7** (return to document) . . . . `F7`

53. Follow steps 1-6 of Create a Primary File on pages 119-121 to place name and address lines.

Example: Primary File
{FIELD}1~ {FIELD}2~ {FIELD}3~
{FIELD}4?~
[FIELD]5~
[FIELD]6~, [FIELD]7~ {FIELD}8~

130

Merge (continued)
Labels (Primary File continued)

54. Press **F7** (Exit) . . . . `F7`

OR	Pull-down Menu	OR
A) Press **Alt + =**		`Alt`+`=`
B) Select **F** (File)		`F`
C) Select **X** (Exit)		`X`

55. Type **Y** (Save document) . . . . `Y`

56. Type document name . . . . Filename

57. **Enter** . . . . `↵`

58. **Enter** . . . . `↵`

Merge (continued)

LABELS (Merged Document)
See Create a Merge Document section.

Example:
Merged Labels (partial)

Mr. Rab Auslander   Mr. Tom River   Joe Smo
Riverdale Shipping   Crab Processing Inc.   123 Wood Blvd.
121 Mariners Drive   124 Crab Pot Drive   Staten Island, NY 10303
Spring, ME 01342   Bayway, NJ, 14222

SAVE MERGED DOCUMENT (Label)

1. Press **F7** (Exit) .... `F7`

OR	Pull-down Menu	OR
A) Press **Alt + =**		`Alt`+`=`
B) Select **F** (File)		`F`
C) Select **X** (Exit)		`X`

2. Type **Y** (Save document) .... `Y`

3. Type document name .... Filename

4. **Enter** .... ⏎

5. **Enter** .... ⏎

NOTE: To print document see Print on pages 19-21.

SEARCH

FORWARD

1. Place cursor BEFORE text to be searched.

2. Press **F2** (⇒Srch) . . . . `F2`

OR	Pull-down Menu	OR
A) Press **Alt + =**		`Alt`+`=`
B) Select **S** (Search)		`S`
C) Select **F** (Forward)		`F`

3. Type search text or codes.

4. Press **F2** (begin search) . . . . `F2`
   NOTE: The cursor stops after first match is found.
5. Press **F2**, twice to repeat search. . . . . . `F2` `F2`

OR	Pull-down Menu	OR
A) Press **Alt + =**		`Alt`+`=`
B) Select **S** (Search)		`S`
C) Select **N** (Next)		`N`

NOTE: Lowercase characters will match both lowercase and UPPERCASE. UPPERCASE will only match UPPERCASE.

Search (continued)

REVERSE SEARCH

1. Place cursor AFTER text to be searched.

2. Press **Shift + F2** (⇐Srch) . . . . `Shift`+`F2`

OR	Pull-down Menu	OR
A) Press **Alt + =**		`Alt`+`=`
B) Select **S** (Search)		`S`
C) Select **B** (Backward)		`B`

3. Type search text or codes.

4. Press **Shift + F2** (⇐Srch) . . . . `Shift`+`F2`

5. Press **Shift + F2**, twice to repeat search . . . . `Shift`+`F2` `Shift`+`F2`

OR	Pull-down Menu	OR
A) Press **Alt + =**		`Alt`+`=`
B) Select **S** (Search)		`S`
C) Select **P** (Previous)		`P`

Search (continued)

EXTENDED SEARCH

Also searches headers, footers, footnotes, and endnotes.

1. Press **Home, F2** (Extended ⇒Srch). `Home` `F2`

   OR   **OR**

   Press **Home, Shift + F2**
   (Extended ⇐Srch) . . . . `Home` `Shift`+`F2`

OR	Pull-down Menu	OR
A) Press **Alt + =**		`Alt`+`=`
B) Select **S** (Search)		`S`
C) Select **E** (Extended)		`E`
D) Select **F** (Forward)		`F`
OR		**OR**
Select **B** (Backward)		`B`

2. Type search text or codes.

3. Press **F2** (Search) . . . . `F2`

OR	Pull-down Menu	OR
A) Press **Alt + =**		`Alt`+`=`
B) Select **S** (Search)		`S`
C) Select **E** (Extended)		`E`
D) Select **N** (Next)		`N`
OR		**OR**
Select **P** (Previous)		`P`

4. Press **Home** . . . . `Home`

5. Press **F2, F2** (repeat Extended ⇒Srch). `F2` `F2`

   OR   **OR**

6. Press **Shift + F2, F2**
   (repeat Extended ⇐Srch) . . . . `Shift`+`F2` `F2`

135

Search (continued)

SEARCH AND REPLACE

1. Press **Alt + F2** (Replace) . . . . `Alt`+`F2`

OR	Pull-down Menu	OR
A) Press **Alt + =**		`Alt`+`=`
B) Select **S** (Search)		`S`
C) Select **R** (Replace)		`R`

2. Type **Y** (confirm each replacement) . . . . `Y`

   OR   OR

   Type **N** (no confirmation) . . . . `N`

3. Type string of characters or codes to be replaced.

4. Press **F2** (⇒Srch) . . . . `F2`

5. Type replacement text and/or codes.

6. Press **F2** (begin replacing) . . . . `F2`

SEARCH AND REPLACE IN A BLOCK

1. Press **Alt + F4** (Block) . . . . `Alt`+`F4`

OR	Pull-down Menu	OR
A) Press **Alt + =**		`Alt`+`=`
B) Select **E** (Edit)		`E`
C) Select **B** (Block)		`B`

2. Highlight text (See Block Text on page 10).

3. Repeat steps 1-6 from Search and Replace above.

SUPER/SUBSCRIPT

*NOTE: Printer must support this feature for
successful printing.*

ONE CHARACTER

1. Place cursor where super/subscript is to be inserted.

2. Press **Ctrl + F8, S** (Font, Size) . `Ctrl`+`F8` `S`

OR	Pull-down Menu	OR
A) Press **Alt + =**		`Alt`+`=`
B) Select **O** (Font)		`O`

3. Select **P** (Suprscpt) .... `P`

   OR   OR

   Select **B** (Subscpt) .... `B`

4. Type text.

5. Press **Right Arrow** .... `→`

   *NOTE: To view Super/Subscript Refer to View
   Document On Screen on page 25.*

BLOCK OF TEXT

1. Press **Alt + F4** (Block) .... `Alt`+`F4`

OR	Pull-down Menu	OR
A) Press **Alt + =**		`Alt`+`=`
B) Select **E** (Edit)		`E`
C) Select **B** (Block)		`B`

2. Highlight text (see Block Text on page 10).

Continued ...

Super/Subscript (continued)
Block of Text (continued)

3. Press **Ctrl + F8, S** (Font, Size) . `Ctrl`+`F8` `S`

OR	Pull-down Menu	OR
A) Press **Alt + =**		`Alt`+`=`
B) Select **O** (Font)		`O`

4. Select **P** (Suprscpt) . . . . `P`

   OR   OR

   Select **B** (Subscpt) . . . . `B`

SPELLER

NOTE: If two disk drives, replace the diskette in Drive B with the speller diskette.

1. Press **Ctrl + F2** (Spell) . . . . `Ctrl`+`F2`

OR	Pull-down Menu	OR
A) Press **Alt + =**		`Alt`+`=`
B) Select **T** (Tools)		`T`
C) Select **E** (Spell)		`E`

2. Select **one** of the following: **Option**

  a) **W** (Word) Check current word . . . . `W`

  b) **P** (Page) Check current page . . . . `P`

  c) **D** (Document) Check entire document . `D`

  d) **N** (New Sup. Dictionary) Use a new supplementary dictionary . . . . `N`

  e) **L** (Look up) Look up a word in the main dictionary that matches a pattern . . . `L`

  f) **C** (Count) - Count number of words . . . `C`

NOTE: Press F1 (Cancel) to stop spell-checking.

138

Speller (continued)

NOT FOUND MENU

1. Select **one** of the following: **Option**

   a) Choose one of the alternative words
      listed by letter (if any are listed) . . . . Letter

   b) **1** (Skip Once) Speller stops at next
      occurrence of the word . . . . **`1`**

   c) **2** (Skip) Word is ignored for rest
      of document . . . . **`2`**

   d) **3** (Add) Word is saved in supplementary
      dictionary . . . . **`3`**

   e) **4** (Edit) Edit word in document. . . . . . . **`4`**

      1) Edit spelling of text.

      2) Press **F7** . . . . **`F7`**

   f) **5** (Look up) Finds words in the main dictionary
      that matches a pattern, and replaces
      misspelled word with the correct spelling.

      1) Type pattern.

   *NOTE: Use a "?" to represent any single character
   or an "*" to represent a any group of
   characters. Example: Type **Part*** to display
   all words that begin with "Part".*

      2) **Enter** . . . . **`⏎`**

      3) Select letter of correct spelling . . . . Letter

DOUBLE WORD MENU

1. Select **one** of the following: **Option**

   a) **1** or **2** (Skip) Double Word
      Checking continues
      to next occurrence . . . . `1` or `2`

   b) **3** (Delete 2nd) Second occurrence of
      word is deleted . . . . `3`

   c) **4** (Edit) . . . . `4`

      1) Edit spelling of text.

      2) Press **F7** . . . . `F7`

   d) **5** (Disable Double Word Checking)
      Double words are ignored . . . . `5`

SPELLER UTILITY

TWO DISK DRIVES
At A>:
1. Place data diskette in
   Drive B.

2. Place Speller Diskette in
   Drive A.

3. Type **Spell**

4. **Enter**

HARD DISK DRIVE
At C>:
1. Change to WordPerfect
   directory that contains
   SPELL.EXE file.

2. Type **Spell**

3. **Enter**

Continued ...

Speller (continued)
Speller Utility (continued)

Select **one** of the following: Option

a) **0** (Exit) Exit Spell Utility **0**

b) **1** (Change/Create Dictionary) Changes
to, or creates another dictionary **1**

c) **2** (Add words to dictionary) **2**

d) **3** (Delete words from dictionary) **3**

e) **4** (Optimize Dictionary) Select this after
creating a new dictionary **4**

f) **5** (Display list of common words) **5**

g) **6** (Check location of a word) **6**

h) **7** (Look up) Check a word pattern **7**

i) **8** (Phonetic Look Up) Searches for
words in dictionary that sounds
like source word **8**

j) **9** (Convert 4.2 Dictionary to 5.1) **9**

k) **A** (Combine other 5.0 or 5.1 Dictionary) **A**

l) **B** (Compress/Expand Supplemental
Dictionary) . . . . **B**

m) **C** (Extract added words from Word
list-based Dictionary) . . . . **C**

THESAURUS

1. Place cursor on word to be looked up.

   NOTE: If Two Disk Drives, replace the diskette in Drive B with Thesaurus diskette.

2. Press **Alt + F1** (Thesaurus) . . . . `Alt`+`F1`

OR	Pull-down Menu	OR
A) Press **Alt + =**		`Alt`+`=`
B) Select **T** (Tools)		`T`
C) Select **H** (Thesaurus)		`H`

   NOTE: Use Left Arrow and Right Arrow to move option letters to desired column. Use Up Arrow and Down Arrow to view portions of columns not on display.

3. Select **one** of the following: Option

   a) **1** (Replace Word) . . . . `1`

      Type letter preceding desired word . . . . Letter

   b) **2** (View Document) . . . . `2`

      1) Move through document.

      2) Press **F7** (return to Thesaurus) . . . . . `F7`

   c) **3** (Look Up Word) . . . . `3`

      1) Type word to be looked up.

      2) **Enter** . . . . `⏎`

   d) **4** (Clear Column) . . . . `4`

Continued ...

142

4. Press **F7** (return to document) ....

Illustration of Screen:

```
┌select—(v)──────────  ┌choose —(v)──────────────────────────
│  1  A  .Choose       │1.   .cull          choose—(ant)—
│     B  .cull         │     .pick          5    .refuse
│     C  .designate    │     .select             .reject
│     D  .pick         │
│     E  .prefer       │2.   .adopt
│                      │     .embrace
│ select—(v)───────    │     .espouse
│  2  F  .choice       │
│     G  .elect        │3.   .decide
│     H  .elite        │     .determine
│     I  .prime        │     .elect
│     J  .superior     │     .perfer
```

OUTLINE

CREATE

1. Create or retrieve document where outline is to be added.

   NOTE: Tabs determine indent values within outline levels.

2. Place cursor where outline is to begin.

3. Press **Shift + F5** (Date/Outline) .... `Shift` + `F5`

OR	Pull-down Menu	OR
A) Press **Alt + =**		`Alt` + `=`
B) Select **T** (Tools)		`T`

4. Select **O** (Outline) .... `O`

5. Select **O** (On) .... `O`

6. **Enter** (reveal outline level one) .... `↵`

7. Press **F4** (Indent) .... `F4`

8. Type text.

9. **Enter** .... `↵`

Continued ...

144

10. Press **Tab** if necessary to increase
    outline level depth .... `Tab`

    *NOTE: Each arrow (→) below represents **Tab**.*

                                        → A.
    Once to reveal sublevel one............. → B.
                                        → etc.

                                        → → 1.
    Twice to reveal sublevel two............. → → 2.
                                        → → etc.

                                        → → → a.
    Three times to reveal sublevel three.. → → → b.
                                        → → → etc.

    *NOTE: **Shift + Tab** (Margin Release) will back
    out of outline levels.*

11. Repeat steps 6-10 until outline is complete.

12. Press **Shift + F5** (Date/Outline) .... `Shift`+`F5`

OR	Pull-down Menu	OR
A) Press **Alt + =**		`Alt`+`=`
B) Select **T** (Tools)		`T`

13. Select **O** (Outline) .... `O`

14. Select **F** (Off) .... `F`

Outline (continued)

REMOVING OUTLINE NUMBERS

1. Place cursor on outline number to be deleted.

2. Press **Del** (delete paragraph code) . . . . `Del`
   *NOTE: Remaining outline numbers are
   automatically renumbered.*

CHANGING OUTLINE NUMBERING STYLES

1. Place cursor where outline style change is to begin.

2. Press **Shift + F5** (Date/Outline) . . . . `Shift`+`F5`

OR	Pull-down Menu	OR
A) Press **Alt + =**		`Alt`+`=`
B) Select **T** (Tools)		`T`

3. Select **D** (Define) . . . . `D`

4. Select **one** of the following: Option

   a) **P** (Paragraph: 1. a. i. (1) (a) (i) 1) a)) . . `P`

   b) **O** (Outline: I. A. 1. a. (1) (a) i) a)) . . . . . `O`

   c) **L** (Legal: 1., 1.1, 1.11, etc.) . . . . `L`

   d) **B** (Bullets: , ○, -, ■, *, •, x) . . . . `B`

   e) **U** (User-Defined) . . . . `U`

5. **Enter** . . . . `↵`

6. Press **F7** (return to document) . . . . `F7`

MOVE OUTLINE FAMILY

An outline family consists of the outline level at the present cursor position.

1. Place cursor on the first line of outline family.

2. Press **Shift + F5** (Date/Outline) .... **Shift** + **F5**

OR	Pull-down Menu	OR
A) Press **Alt + =**		**Alt** + **=**
B) Select **T** (Tools)		**T**

3. Select **O** (Outline) .... **O**

4. Select **M** (Move family) .... **M**

5. Use cursor movement keys to move highlighted outline family.

6. **Enter** .... **↵**

COPY OUTLINE FAMILY

1. Place cursor on the first line of outline family.

2. Press **Shift + F5** (Date/Outline) .... **Shift** + **F5**

OR	Pull-down Menu	OR
A) Press **Alt + =**		**Alt** + **=**
B) Select **T** (Tools)		**T**

3. Select **O** (Outline) .... **O**

4. Select **C** (Copy family) .... **C**

5. Use cursor movement keys to move highlighted outline family.

6. **Enter** .... **↵**

Outline (continued)

DELETE OUTLINE FAMILY

1. Place cursor on the first line of outline family.

2. Press **Shift + F5** (Date/Outline) .... `Shift` + `F5`

OR	Pull-down Menu	OR
A) Press **Alt + =**		`Alt` + `=`
B) Select **T** (Tools)		`T`

3. Select **O** (Outline) .... `O`

4. Select **D** (Delete family) .... `D`

5. Type **Y** (Delete Outline Family) .... `Y`

6. **Enter** .... `↵`

CREATE OUTLINE STYLE

Note: Outline styles provide increased and automated control of the format of text in each level of the outline.

1. Press **Shift + F5** (Date/Outline) .... `Shift` + `F5`

OR	Pull-down Menu	OR
A) Press **Alt + =**		`Alt` + `=`
B) Select **T** (Tools)		`T`

2. Select **D** (Define) .... `D`

3. Select **N** (Outline style Name) .... `N`

4. Select **C** (Create) .... `C`

5. Select **N** (Name) .... `N`

Continued ...

148

Outline (continued)
Create Outline Style (continued)

6. Type name of new style . . . . Stylename

7. Select **D** (Description) . . . . `D`

8. Type style description.

9. For each outline level:

   a) Place cursor on level number.

   b) Select **T** (Type) . . . . `T`

   c) Select **P** (Paired) . . . . `P`

   OR   OR

   Select **O** (Open) . . . . `O`

   d) Select **C** (Codes) . . . . `C`

   e) Insert codes and text as desired.

   Example: Tab codes before Paragraph # code
   and Indent code after it.
   [Tab][Tab][**Par Num:2**][Indent]

10. Press **F7** . . . . `F7`

11. Press **F7** . . . . `F7`

12. Press **F7** . . . . `F7`

13. Press **F7** (return to document) . . . . `F7`

Outline (continued)

USE AN OUTLINE STYLE

1. Press **Shift + F5** (Date/Outline) .... |Shift| + |F5|

OR	Pull-down Menu	OR
A) Press **Alt + =**		|Alt| + |=|
B) Select **T** (Tools)		|T|

2. Select **D** (Define) .... |D|

3. Select **N** (Outline style Name) .... |N|

4. Select **C** (Create) .... |C|

5. Select **N** (Name) .... |N|

6. Use cursor movement keys to highlight desired outline style.

7. **Enter** .... |←|

8. Press **F7** (exit to Date/Outline menu) .... |F7|

9. Select **O** (Outline) .... |O|

10. Select **O** (On) .... |O|

> *NOTE:* *Key text and establish levels as you would for regular outline mode. See Create Outline on pages 143 and 144.*

150
DATE

TEXT

Computer's "system" date will permanently appear in document.

1. Press **Shift + F5** (Date/Outline) .... `Shift`+`F5`

OR	Pull-down Menu	OR
A) Press **Alt + =**		`Alt`+`=`
B) Select **T** (Tools)		`T`

2. Select **T** (Date **T**ext) .... `T`

CODE

Date Code will update to computer's "system" date each time the document is edited or printed.

1. Press **Shift + F5** (Date/Outline) .... `Shift`+`F5`

OR	Pull-down Menu	OR
A) Press **Alt + =**		`Alt`+`=`
B) Select **T** (Tools)		`T`

2. Select **C** (Date **C**ode) .... `C`

LIST FILES

(Use with Retrieve, Delete, Move/Rename, Print,
Short/Long Display, Look, Other Directory, Copy,
Find, and Name Search.)

1. Press F5 (List Files) . . . . `F5`

OR	Pull-down Menu	OR
A) Press Alt + = ...		`Alt`+`=`
B) Select F (File)		`F`
C) Select F (List Files)		`F`

NOTE: Indicate drive and/or directory if necessary.
2. **Enter** . . . . `↵`

3. Use cursor movement keys to highlight desired
   document.

4. Select **one** of the following: Option

   a) **R** (Retrieve) . . . . `R`

   b) **D** (Delete) . . . . `D`

   Type **Y** (to confirm deletion) . . . . `Y`

   c) **M** (Move/Rename) . . . . `M`

   1) Type new document name . . . . . Filename

   2) **Enter** . . . . `↵`

   d) **P** (Print) . . . . `P`

   1) Type page numbers if not entire document.

   2) **Enter** . . . . `↵`

*NOTE: Type "y" if WordPerfect indicates that the
document needs to be generated. This
message usually indicates that the
document was previously formatted for
another printer.*

Continued ...

152

List Files (continued)

Option

e) **S** (Short/Long display) . . . . ⬛**S**

   1) Select **S** (Short Display) . . . . ⬛**S**

     OR   **OR**

     Select **L** (Long Display) . . . . ⬛**L**

   2) **Enter** . . . . ⏎

f) **L** (Look) . . . . ⬛**L**

   1) Select **N** (Next Document) . . . . ⬛**N**

     OR   **OR**

     Select **P** (Previous Document) . . . . . ⬛**P**

   2) Press **F7** (return to List Files) . . . . . . ⬛**F7**

g) **O** (Other Directory) . . . . ⬛**O**

   1) Type new directory name.   Directory name

     OR

     Highlight desired directory.

   2) **Enter** . . . . ⏎

h) **C** (Copy) . . . . ⬛**C**

   1) Type name of new document or
     target document.

   2) **Enter** . . . . ⏎

Continued ...

List Files (continued)

Option

i) **F** (Find) . . . . **F**

Select **one** of the following: Option

1) **N** (Name) . . . . **N**

a. Type word pattern.

b. **Enter** . . . . **↵**

NOTE: *Remaining documents contain*
specified word pattern.

c. Press **F7** **F7**
(return to List Files)

2) **D** (Doc Summary) . . . . **D**

a. Type word pattern.

b. **Enter** . . . . **↵**

NOTE: *Remaining documents contain*
specified word pattern.

c. Press **F7** **F7**
(return to List Files)

3) **P** (First Pg.) . . . . **P**

a. Type word pattern.

b. **Enter** . . . . **↵**

NOTE: *Remaining documents contain*
specified word pattern.

c. Press **F7** **F7**
(return to List Files)

Continued ...

List Files (continued)
Find (continued)

Option

4) **E** (Entire Doc) . . . . 🇪

   a. Type word pattern.

   b. **Enter** . . . . ↵

NOTE: *Remaining documents contain*
       specified word pattern.
   c. Press **F7** (return to List Files) F7

5) **C** (Conditions) C

   a. Type search conditions.

   b. **Enter** . . . . ↵

NOTE: *Remaining documents contain*
       search conditions.
   c. Press **F7** (return to List Files) F7

6) **N** (Name Search) . . . . N

   a. Type document name . . . . . . Filename

   b. Press **F7** (return to document) . . F7

DOCUMENT COMMENTS

CREATE

1. Place cursor on line where comment is to appear.

2. Press **Ctrl + F5** (Text In/Out) . . . . `Ctrl`+`F5`

3. Select **C** (Comment) . . . . `C`

OR	Pull-down Menu	OR
A) Press **Alt + =**		`Alt`+`=`
B) Select **E** (Edit)		`E`
C) Select **O** (Comment)		`O`

4. Select **C** (Create) . . . . `C`

5. Type comment.

6. Press **F7** (return to document) . . . . `F7`
   NOTE: Comments cannot be used in columns.

EDIT

1. Press **Alt + F3** (Reveal Codes) to verify
   position in document . . . . `Alt`+`F3`

OR	Pull-down Menu	OR
A) Press **Alt + =**		`Alt`+`=`
B) Select **E** (Edit)		`E`
C) Select **R** (Reveal Codes)		`R`

2. Place cursor to right of comment to be edited.

3. Press **Ctrl + F5** (Text In/Out) . . . . `Ctrl`+`F5`

Continued ...

Document Comments (continued)
Edit (continued)

4. Select **C** (Comment) . . . . `C`

OR	Pull-down Menu	OR
A) Press **Alt + =**		`Alt`+`=`
B) Select **E** (Edit)		`E`
C) Select **O** (Comment)		`O`

5. Select **E** (Edit) . . . . `E`

6. Edit comment.

7. Press **F7** (return to document) . . . . `F7`

DISPLAY COMMENTS

1. Press **Shift + F1** (Setup) . . . . `Shift`+`F1`

OR	Pull-down Menu	OR
A) Press **Alt + =**		`Alt`+`=`
B) Select **F** (File)		`F`
C) Select **T** (Setup)		`T`

2. Select **D** (Display) . . . . `D`

3. Select **E** (E-Screen Options) . . . . `E`

4. Select **C** (Comments Display) . . . . `C`

5. Type **Y** . . . . `Y`

    OR   OR

    Type **N** . . . . `N`

6. Press **F7** (return to document) . . . . `F7`

REDLINE TEXT

1 Retrieve document to be edited.

2. Press **Ctrl + F8** (Font) . . . . `Ctrl` + `F8`

OR	Pull-down Menu	OR
A) Press **Alt + =**		`Alt` + `=`
B) Select **O** (Font)		`O`

3. Select **A** (Appearance) . . . . `A`

4. Select **R** (Redline) . . . . `R`

5. Type text to be Redlined.

6. Press **Right Arrow** (end Redline) . . . . `→`
   NOTE: Text is printed with "redline" background.

BLOCK OF TEXT

1. Retrieve document to be edited.

2. Place cursor on first character to be redlined.

3. Press **Alt + F4** (Block) . . . . `Alt` + `F4`

OR	Pull-down Menu	OR
A) Press **Alt + =**		`Alt` + `=`
B) Select **E** (Edit)		`E`
C) Select **B** (Block)		`B`

4. Highlight text (See Block Text on page 10).

Continued ...

Redline Text (continued)
Block of Text (continued)

5. Press **Ctrl + F8** (Font) . . . . `Ctrl`+`F8`

OR	Pull-down Menu	OR
A) Press **Alt + =**		`Alt`+`=`
B) Select **O** (Font)		`O`

6. Select **A** (Appearance) . . . . `A`

7. Select **R** (Redline) . . . . `R`

STRIKEOUT TEXT

1. Retrieve document to be edited.

2. Place cursor on first character of text to be deleted.

3. Press **Alt + F4** (Block) . . . . `Alt`+`F4`

OR	Pull-down Menu	OR
A) Press **Alt + =**		`Alt`+`=`
B) Select **E** (Edit)		`E`
C) Select **B** (Block)		`B`

4. Highlight text (See Block Text on page 10).

5. Press **Ctrl + F8** (Font) . . . . `Ctrl`+`F8`

OR	Pull-down Menu	OR
A) Press **Alt + =**		`Alt`+`=`
B) Select **O** (Font)		`O`

6. Select **A** (Appearance) . . . . `A`

7. Select **S** (Strikeout) . . . . `S`

Strikeout Text (continued)

REMOVE REDLINE AND STRIKEOUT

1. Retrieve document to be edited.

2. Press **Alt + F5** (Mark Text) . . . . `Alt` + `F5`

OR	Pull-down Menu	OR
A) Press **Alt + =**		`Alt` + `=`
B) Select **M** (Mark)		`M`

3. Select **G** (Generate) . . . . `G`

4. Select **R** (Remove Redline and Strikeout) . . . . . `R`

5. Type **Y** (confirm deletions) . . . . `Y`

TAB RULER

1. Retrieve document.

2. Press **Ctrl + F3** (Screen) . . . . `Ctrl` + `F3`

OR	Pull-down Menu	OR
A) Press **Alt + =**		`Alt` + `=`
B) Select **E** (Edit)		`E`

3. Select **W** (Window) . . . . `W`

4. Press **Up Arrow** . . . . `↑`

5. **Enter** (Tab Ruler in place) . . . . `↵`

160

REMOVE TAB RULER

1. Press **Ctrl + F3** (Screen) . . . . `Ctrl`+`F3`

OR	Pull-down Menu	OR
A) Press **Alt + =**		`Alt`+`=`
B) Select **E** (Edit)		`E`

2. Select **W** (Window) . . . . `W`

3. Type **24** . . . . `2` `4`

4. Enter . . . . `⏎`

SPLIT SCREEN (WINDOWS)

VIEW TWO DOCUMENTS AT ONCE

1. Retrieve first document.

2. Press **Ctrl + F3** (Screen) . . . . `Ctrl`+`F3`

OR	Pull-down Menu	OR
A) Press **Alt + =**		`Alt`+`=`
B) Select **E** (Edit)		`E`

3. Select **W** (Window) . . . . `W`

4. Type number of lines wanted to be displayed for current window (maximum 20 lines) . . . . . . Number

   OR   **OR**

   Press **Up Arrow** to move Tab Ruler to desired position . . . . `↑`

5. **Enter** (set Window) . . . . `⏎`

Continued ...

Split Screen (continued)

6. Press **Shift + F3** (Switch) .... [Shift]+[F3]

OR	Pull-down Menu	OR
A) Press **Alt + =**		[Alt]+[=]
B) Select **E** (Edit)		[E]
C) Select **S** (Switch)		[S]

7. Retrieve second document.

8. Press **Shift + F3** (Switch) .... [Shift]+[F3]

OR	Pull-down Menu	OR
A) Press **Alt + =**		[Alt]+[=]
B) Select **E** (Edit)		[E]
C) Select **S** (Switch)		[S]

CLOSE WINDOW

1. Press **Ctrl + F3** (Screen) .... [Ctrl]+[F3]

OR	Pull-down Menu	OR
A) Press **Alt + =**		[Alt]+[=]
B) Select **E** (Edit)		[E]

2. Select **W** (Window) .... [W]

3. Type **24** .... [2][4]

4. **Enter** (close Window) .... [↵]

SAVE AND EXIT SECOND DOCUMENT

1. Place cursor in window of second document.

2. Press **F7** (Exit) . . . . `F7`

3. **Enter** . . . . `⏎`

4. If document is saved:

   a) **Enter** . . . . `⏎`

   b) Type **Y** (replace document) . . . . `Y`

   OR   **OR**

   To save document:

   a) Type document name . . . . Filename

   b) **Enter** . . . . `⏎`

5. Type **Y** (Exit second document) . . . . `Y`

SWITCH DOCUMENTS

EDIT TWO DOCUMENTS AT THE SAME TIME

   *NOTE: Each window is a separate editing screen
   with its own status line.*

1. Retrieve first document to be edited.

2. Press **Shift + F3** (Switch) . . . . `Shift`+`F3`

OR	Pull-down Menu	OR
A) Press **Alt + =**		`Alt`+`=`
B) Select **E** (Edit)		`E`
C) Select **S** (Switch)		`S`

   *NOTE: "Doc 2" appears on the status line
   indicating second document.*

Continued ...

163

Switch Documents (continued)
Edit Two Documents at the Same Time (continued)

3. Retrieve second document to be edited.

4. Edit documents.

MACROS

CREATE/REPLACE

1. Press **Ctrl + F10** (Macro Define) ....

OR	Pull-down Menu	OR
A) Press **Alt + =**		**Alt** + **=**
B) Select **T** (Tools)		**T**
C) Select **A** (Macro)		**A**
D) Select **D** (Define)		**D**

2. Select **one** of the following: **Option**

   a) **Enter** (no name) ....

   b) Type macro name:

      1) Type name
      (maximum 8 characters) ... Macroname

      2) **Enter** ....

      3) Type description.

      4) **Enter** ....

   c) Press **Alt + a letter A-Z** .....

      1) Type description.

      2) **Enter** ....

3. Type keystrokes to be recorded.

Continued ...

Macros (continued)
Create/Replace (continued)

4. Press **Ctrl + F10** . . . . `Ctrl`+`F10`
   (end macro definition)

OR	Pull-down Menu	OR
A) Press **Alt + =**		`Alt`+`=`
B) Select **T** (Tools)		`T`
C) Select **A** (Macro)		`A`
D) Select **D** (Define)		`D`

PAUSE

1. Follow steps 1-3 of Macros from previous page.

2. Press **Ctrl + PgUp** . . . . `Ctrl`+`PgUp`
   (Macro Commands)

3. Select **P** (Pause) . . . . `P`

4. Continue defining macro.

5. Press **Ctrl + F10** . . . . `Ctrl`+`F10`
   (end macro definition)

Macros (continued)

PLAYBACK

1. Place cursor where macro is to be executed.

   *NOTE: If macro was named using the Alt key,
   press Alt key and letter to execute macro.
   If macro was created without a name
   (only a return) then skip step 3.*

2. Press **Alt + F10** (Macro) .... Alt + F10

OR	Pull-down Menu	OR
A) Press **Alt + =**		Alt + =
B) Select **T** (Tools)		T
C) Select **A** (Macro)		A
D) Select **X** (Execute)		X

3. Type macro name. .... Macroname

4. **Enter** ....

   If pause was created:

   a) Type desired text when macro pauses.

   b) **Enter** (to continue playback) ....

STOPPING MACRO

Press F1 (Cancel) to stop Macro playback. F1

166

EDIT MACRO

1. Press **Ctrl + F10** (Macro) . . . . `Ctrl` + `F10`

OR	Pull-down Menu	OR
A) Press **Alt + =**		`Alt` + `=`
B) Select **T** (Tools)		`T`
C) Select **A** (Macro)		`A`
D) Select **D** (Define)		`D`

2. Type macro name . . . . Macroname
   NOTE: If macro was named using the Alt key, skip step 3.
3. **Enter** . . . . `↵`
4. Select **E** (Edit) . . . . `E`
5. Select **D** (Description) . . . . `D`
6. Edit description.
7. **Enter** . . . . `↵`
8. Edit macro.
   NOTE: Pressing Ctrl + PgUp displays the selection of the Macro Commands.
9. Press **F7** (return to document) . . . . `F7`

ESCAPE
> *NOTE: This will repeat a function or character a specified number of times.*

1. Place cursor where repetition is to begin.

2. Press **Esc** (Repeat Value = 8) . . . . `Esc`

Change Repetition Value (Option)

    a) Type repetition value . . . . Number

    b) **Enter** . . . . `⏎`

3. Select **one** of the following: **Option**

    Arrow Keys . . . . `←` `→` `↑` `↓`

    Delete Word . . . . `Ctrl`+`BkSp`

    Delete Line . . . . `Ctrl`+`End`

    Macro . . . . `Alt`+`F10`

        a) Type macro name . . . . Macroname

        b) **Enter** . . . . `⏎`

    Word Left . . . . `Ctrl`+`←`

    Word Right . . . . `Ctrl`+`→`

168

LINE DRAW

NOTE: Printer must support this procedure for successful printing.

1. Place cursor on line where drawing is to begin.

2. Press **Ctrl + F3** (Screen) . . . . `Ctrl`+`F3`

OR	Pull-down Menu	OR
A) Press **Alt + =**		`Alt`+`=`
B) Select **T** (Tools)		`T`

3. Select **L** (Line Draw) . . . . `L`

4. Select **one** of the following: Option

   a) **1** (Single line |) . . . . `1`

   b) **2** (Double line ‖) . . . . `2`

   c) **3** (Asterisk *) . . . . `3`

   d) **C** (Change) . . . . `C`

*NOTE: Allows user to specify character, fill pattern or thickness to replace option 3 (Asterisk *)*

   e) **E** (Erase) . . . . `E`

   f) **M** (Move) . . . . `M`

5. Use cursor movement keys to create drawing.

6. Press **F7** (return to document) . . . . `F7`

SORT

SINGLE LINE SORT

1. Press **Ctrl + F9** (Merge/Sort) .... `Ctrl` + `F9`

OR	Pull-down Menu	OR
A) Press **Alt + =**		`Alt` + `=`
B) Select **T** (Tools)		`T`

2. Select **S** (Sort) .... `S`

3. Type name of source document .... Filename

4. **Enter** .... `↵`

5. Type name of target document .... Filename

6. **Enter** .... `↵`

7. Select **T** (Type) .... `T`

8. Select **L** (Line) .... `L`

9. Select **K** (Keys) .... `K`

10. Define key.

   NOTE: The default setting for key1 cannot be deleted.

   Example: Key 1 = Type: **a** (alphanumeric)
   Field: **1**
   Word: **2**

   or

   Key 2 = Type: **n** (numeric)
   Field: **3**
   Word: **1**

Continued ...

Sort (continued)

SINGLE LINE SORT (continued)

Illustration of Screen:

--- Sort by Line ---											
Key	Typ	Field	Word	Key	Typ	Field	Word	Key	Typ	Field	Word
→1	a	1	2	2				3			
4				5				6			
7				8				9			
Select											

Action	Order	Type
Sort	Ascending	Line sort

Illustration of Screen:

--- Sort by Line ---											
Key	Typ	Field	Word	Key	Typ	Field	Word	Key	Typ	Field	Word
→1	n	3	1	2				3			
4				5				6			
7				8				9			
Select											

Action	Order	Type
Sort	Ascending	Line sort

11. Press **F7** (Exit keys) . . . . `F7`

12. Select **O** (Order) . . . . `O`

13. Select **A** (Ascending) . . . . `A`

    OR   OR

    Select **D** (Descending) . . . . `D`

14. Select **P** (Perform Action) . . . . `P`

Sort (continued)

MULTIPLE LINE SORT

1. Follow steps 1-9 of Single line on page 169.

2. Define Keys (up to nine keys can be defined).

Example: Key 1 = Type: **a** (alphanumeric)
             Field: **4**
             Word: **1**
        Key 2 = Type: **n** (numeric)
             Field: **2**
             Word: **1**
        Key 3 = Type: **a** (alphanumeric)
             Field: **1**
             Word: **2**

Illustration of Screen:

```
----------------------------- Sort by Line -----------------------------
Key  Typ Field Word      Key  Typ Field Word      Key Typ Field Word
→1   a    4    1          2   n    2    1           3   a    1    2
 4                        5                         6
 7                        8                         9
Select

Action                   Order                     Type
Sort                     Ascending                 Line sort
```

3. Press **F7** (Exit Keys) . . . . 　**F7**

4. Select **O** (Order) . . . . 　**O**

5. Select **A** (Ascending) . . . . 　**A**

   OR　　　　　　　　　　　　　　　　　　　　　　　**OR**

   Select **D** (Descending) . . . . 　**D**

6. Select **P** (Perform Action) . . . . 　**P**

   *NOTE: To view sorted records saved in a new
           document, retrieve target document.*

MERGE SORT (Secondary merge file)

1. Press **Ctrl + F9** (Merge/Sort) .... `Ctrl` + `F9`

OR	Pull-down Menu	OR
A) Press **Alt + =**		`Alt` + `=`
B) Select **T** (Tools)		`T`

2. Select **S** (Sort) .... `S`

3. Type name of source document .... Filename

4. **Enter** .... `↵`

5. Type name of target document to receive sorted records .... Filename

6. **Enter** .... `↵`

7. Select **T** (Type) .... `T`

8. Select **M** (Merge) .... `M`

9. Select **K** (Keys) .... `K`

10. Press **Delete** (delete key definitions after Key1) `Del`

11. Define Key(s).

   Example: Key 1 = Type: **n** (numeric)
   Field: **7**
   Line: **1**
   Word: **1**

Illustration of Screen:

---------------------------- Sort Secondary Merge File ----------------------------

Key	Typ	Field	Line	Word	Key	Typ	Field	Line	Word	Key	Typ	Field	Line	Word
→1	n	7	1	1	2					3				

Continued ...

Sort (continued)
Merge Sort (Secondary File, continued)

12. Press F7 (Exit Keys) . . . . `F7`

13. Select O (Order) . . . . `O`

14. Select A (Ascending) . . . . `A`

   OR   **OR**

   Select D (Descending) . . . . `D`

15. Select P (Perform Action) . . . . `P`

SELECT ONLY

1. Press Ctrl + F9 (Merge/Sort) . . . . `Ctrl` + `F9`

OR	Pull-down Menu	OR
A) Press Alt + = ...		`Alt` + `=`
B) Select T (Tools)		`T`

2. Select S (Sort) . . . . `S`

3. Type name of source document . . . . Filename

4. **Enter** . . . . `↵`

5. Type name of target document . . . . Filename

6. **Enter** . . . . `↵`

7. Select T (Type) . . . . `T`

   Select **one** of the following: Option

   a) **M** (Merge) . . . . `M`

   b) **L** (Line) . . . . `L`

   c) **P** (Paragraph) . . . . `P`

8. Select K (Keys) . . . . `K`

Continued ...

174

Sort (continued)
Select Only (continued)

9. Press **Delete** (delete key definitions after Key1)

10. Define key(s).

11. Press **F7** (Exit Keys) . . . .

12. Select **S** (Select) . . . . **S**

13. Press **Ctrl + End**
    (delete existing select statement(s)) . .

14. Create select statement.

   Example: Key1=Mr

   or

   Key1=Hawaii

   *NOTE: Select statements can also be created
   using the following symbols:*

   a) **+**   (OR) Use to connect two key definitions
                    when either one must be met.

   b) *****   (AND) Use to connect two key definitions
                    when both must be met.

   c) **=**   (EQUAL)

   d) **< >**   (NOT EQUAL)

   e) **>**   (GREATER THAN)

   f) **<**   (LESS THAN)

   g) **> =**   (GREATER THAN OR EQUAL)

   h) **< =**   (LESS THAN OR EQUAL)

   Example: key1=Ms*key2=Smith

Continued ...

Sort (continued)
Select Only (continued)

15. Press **F7** (Exit Select menu) . . . . `F7`

16. Select **A** (Action) . . . . `A`

17. Select **O** (Select Only) . . . . `O`

18. Select **P** (Perform Action) . . . . `P`

GLOBAL SELECT

Request all records containing key words.
1. Follow steps 1-13 of Select Only (previous) section.

2. Type the select statement using a "g" after the key.
   Example: Keyg=Boston
   *NOTE: With "global select" do not type a key
   number.*

3. Press **F7** (Exit Select) . . . . `F7`

4. Select **A** (Action) . . . . `A`

5. Select **O** (Select Only) . . . . `O`

6. Select **P** (Perform Action) . . . . `P`

SORT AND SELECT (Single and Multiple Lines)

1. Press **Ctrl + F9** (Merge/Sort) . . . . `Ctrl`+`F9`

OR	Pull-down Menu	OR
A) Press **Alt + =**		`Alt`+`=`
B) Select **T** (Tools)		`T`

2. Select **S** (Sort) . . . . `S`

3. Type name of source document . . . . Filename

4. Enter . . . . `↵`

Continued ...

176

Sort (continued)
Sort and Select (continued)

5. Type name of target document . . . . Filename

6. **Enter** . . . . ↵

7. Select **T** (Type) . . . . `T`

8. Select **L** (Line) . . . . `L`

9. Select **K** (Keys) . . . . `K`

10. Define key(s).
    NOTE: Keys must be defined before setting select statement.

11. Press **F7** (Exit Keys) . . . . `F7`

12. Select **S** (Select) . . . . `S`

13. Type select statement.
    (See step 14 of Select Only on page 174.)

14. Press **F7** (Exit Select) . . . . `F7`

15. Select **O** (Order) . . . . `O`

16. Select **A** (Ascending) . . . . `A`

    OR   OR

    Select **D** (Descending) . . . . `D`

17. Select **A** (Action) . . . . `A`

18. Select **S** (Select and Sort) . . . . `S`

19. Select **P** (Perform Action) . . . . `P`

Sort (continued)

SORT AND SELECT (Secondary merge file)

1. Press **Ctrl + F9** (Merge/Sort) . . . . **Ctrl** + **F9**

2. Select **S** (Sort) . . . . **S**

3. Type name of source document . . . . Filename

4. **Enter** . . . . **⏎**

5. Type name of target document . . . . Filename

6. **Enter** . . . . **⏎**

7. Select **T** (Type) . . . . **T**

8. Select **M** (Merge) . . . . **M**

9. Select **K** (Keys) . . . . **K**

10. Define Key(s).

11. Press **F7** (Exit Keys) **F7**

12. Select **S** (Select) . . . . **S**

13. Type select statement
(See step 14 of Select Only on page 174.)

14. Press **F7** (Exit Select) **F7**

15. Select **O** (Order) . . . . **O**

16. Select **A** (Ascending) . . . . **A**

    OR   OR

    Select **D** (Descending) . . . . **D**

17. Select **A** (Action) . . . . **A**

18. Select **S** (Select and Sort) . . . . **S**

19. Select **P** (Perform Action) . . . . **P**

TABLE OF CONTENTS

1. Place cursor on first character of text to be marked for Table of Contents.

2. Press **Alt + F4** (Block) . . . . `Alt` + `F4`

OR	Pull-down Menu	OR
A) Press **Alt + =**		`Alt` + `=`
B) Select **E** (Edit)		`E`
C) Select **B** (Block)		`B`

3. Highlight text (see Block Text on page 10).

4. Press **Alt + F5** (Mark Text) . . . . `Alt` + `F5`

OR	Pull-down Menu	OR
A) Press **Alt + =**		`Alt` + `=`
B) Select **M** (Mark)		`M`

5. Select **C** (Table of Contents) . . . . `C`

6. Type level for Table of Contents . . . . Number

7. **Enter** . . . . `↵`

8. Repeat steps 1-7 for each item to be included in table.

9. Press **Ctrl + Home** (Go To) . . . . . . `Ctrl` + `Home`

OR	Pull-down Menu	OR
A) Press **Alt + =**		`Alt` + `=`
B) Select **S** (Search)		`S`
C) Select **G** (Go To)		`G`

10. Press **Home, Home** . . . . `Home` `Home`

11. Press **Up Arrow** . . . . `↑`

Continued ...

Table of Contents (continued)

12. Press **Ctrl + Enter** (HPg) . . . . `Ctrl` + `↵`

13. Press **Left Arrow** . . . . `←`

14. Press **Shift + F6** (Center) . . . . `Shift` + `F6`

15. Type title of Table of Contents.

16. Press **Enter**, twice . . . . `↵` `↵`

17. Press **Alt + F5** (Mark Text) . . . . `Alt` + `F5`

OR	Pull-down Menu	OR
A) Press **Alt + =**		`Alt` + `=`
B) Select **M** (Mark)		`M`

18. Select **D** (Define) . . . . `D`

19. Select **C** (Table of Contents) . . . . `C`

20. Select **N** (Number of Levels) . . . . `N`

21. Type number . . . . Number

22. Press **Enter, Enter** . . . . `↵` `↵`

23. Press **Alt + F5** (Mark Text) . . . . `Alt` + `F5`

OR	Pull-down Menu	OR
A) Press **Alt + =**		`Alt` + `=`
B) Select **M** (Mark)		`M`

24. Select **G** (Generate) . . . . `G`

25. Select **G** . . . . `G`

24. **Enter** . . . . `↵`

25. Type **Y** (replace existing table) . . . . `Y`

180
INDEX (CONCORDANCE)

1. Clear screen (see Clear Screen on page 8).

2. Type first word(s) for index.

3. **Enter** . . . . **⏎**

4. Repeat steps 2-3 for all words to be in index.

5. Press **F7** (Exit) **F7**

OR	Pull-down Menu	OR
A) Press **Alt + =**		**Alt** + **=**
B) Select **F** (File)		**F**
C) Select **X** (Exit)		**X**

6. Type **Y** (save document) . . . . **Y**

7. Type document name (concordance) . . . . Filename

8. **Enter** . . . . **⏎**

9. Type **N** (remain in WordPerfect) . . . . **N**

10. Retrieve document which will contain index.

11. Press **Ctrl + Home** (Go To) . . . . . . **Ctrl** + **Home**

OR	Pull-down Menu	OR
A) Press **Alt + =**		**Alt** + **=**
B) Select **S** (Search)		**S**
C) Select **G** (Go To)		**G**

12. Press **Home, Home** . . . . **Home** **Home**

13. Press **Down Arrow** . . . . **↓**

14. Press **Ctrl + Enter** (HPg) . . . . **Ctrl** + **⏎**

15. Press **Shift + F6** (Center) . . . . **Shift** + **F6**

Continued ...

Index (Concordance continued)

16. Type Title of index.

17. Press **Enter**, twice .... ⏎ ⏎

18. Press **Alt + F5** (Mark Text) .... Alt + F5

OR	Pull-down Menu	OR
A) Press **Alt + =**		Alt + =
B) Select **M** (Mark)		M

19. Select **D** (Define) .... D

20. Select **I** (Index) I

21. Type name of concordance document .. Filename

22. **Enter** .... ⏎

23. Select **one** of the following: Option

   a) **N** (No Page Numbers) .... N

   b) **P** (Page Numbers Follow Entries) ..... P

   c) **(** ((Page Numbers) Follow Entries) ..... (

   d) **F** (Flush Right Page Numbers) .... F

   e) **L** (Flush Right Page Numbers w. Leaders] L

24. Press **Alt + F5** (Mark Text) .... Alt + F5

OR	Pull-down Menu	OR
A) Press **Alt + =**		Alt + =
B) Select **M** (Mark)		M

25. Select **G** (Generate) .... G

26. Select **G** .... G

27. Type **Y** (replace existing index) .... Y

AUTOMATIC REFERENCE

1. Place cursor on line where reference will be inserted.

2. Type reference phrase with a space after the last word.
   Example: "See Bar chart, page "

3. Press **Alt + F5** (Mark Text) . . . . `Alt`+`F5`

OR	Pull-down Menu	OR
A) Press **Alt + =**		`Alt`+`=`
B) Select **M** (Mark)		`M`

4. Select **R** (Cross **R**eference) . . . . `R`

5. Select **R** (Automatic **R**eference) . . . . `R`

6. Select **one** of the following: Option

   a) **P** (**P**age Number) . . . . `P`

   b) **O** (Paragraph/**O**utline Number) . . . . `O`

   c) **F** (**F**ootnote Number) . . . . `F`

   d) **E** (**E**ndnote Number) . . . . `E`

   e) **G** (**G**raphics Box Number) . . . . `G`

7. Type target name . . . . Target name

8. **Enter** . . . . `⏎`

9. Place cursor on target.

10. Press **Alt + F5** (Mark Text) . . . . `Alt`+`F5`

OR	Pull-down Menu	OR
A) Press **Alt + =**		`Alt`+`=`
B) Select **M** (Mark)		`M`

Continued ...

Automatic Reference (continued)

11. Select **R** (Automatic Reference) . . . . `R`

12. Select **T** (Target) . . . . `T`

13. Type target name . . . . Target name

14. **Enter** . . . . `↵`

15. Press **Alt + F5** (Mark Text) . . . . `Alt`+`F5`

OR	Pull-down Menu	OR
A) Press **Alt + =**		`Alt`+`=`
B) Select **M** (Mark)		`M`

16. Select **G** (Generate) . . . . `G`

17. Select **G** . . . . `G`

18. **Enter** . . . . `↵`

FONTS

CHANGING THE BASE FONT

1. Place cursor where font change will begin.

2. Press **Ctrl + F8** (Font) . . . . `Ctrl`+`F8`

OR	Pull-down Menu	OR
A) Press **Alt + =**		`Alt`+`=`
B) Select **O** (Font)		`O`

3. Select **F** (Base Font) . . . . `F`

4. Use cursor movement keys to highlight desired font.

5. Select **S** (Select) . . . . `S`

Fonts (continued)
Changing the Base font

CHANGING FONT SIZE

BEFORE TYPING TEXT

1. Place cursor where font size change will begin.

2. Press **Ctrl + F8** (Font) . . . . **Ctrl** + **F8**

OR	Pull-down Menu	OR
A) Press **Alt + =**		**Alt** + **=**
B) Select **O** (Font)		**O**

---

3. Select **S** (Size) . . . . **S**

4. Select **one** of the following: **Option**

   a) **P** (Superscript) . . . . **P**

   b) **B** (Subscript) . . . . **B**

   c) **F** (Fine) . . . . **F**

   d) **S** (Small) . . . . **S**

   e) **L** (Large) . . . . **L**

   f) **V** (Very Large) . . . . **V**

   g) **E** (Extra Large) . . . . **E**

   *NOTE: Sizes are relative to the base font, and
   depend on what fonts are available for
   printer. If a size is unavailable, the
   closest available size will be substituted.*

5. Type text.

6. Press **Right Arrow** (restore original font setting)

Fonts (continued)

CHANGING FONT SIZE (continued)

EXISTING TEXT

1. Place cursor on first character of text to be changed.

2. Press **Alt + F4** (Block) . . . . **Alt** + **F4**

OR	Pull-down Menu	OR
A) Press **Alt + =**		**Alt** + **=**
B) Select **E** (Edit)		**E**
C) Select **B** (Block)		**B**

3. Highlight text (See Block Text on page 10).

4. Press **Ctrl + F8** (Font) . . . . **Ctrl** + **F8**

OR	Pull-down Menu	OR
A) Press **Alt + =**		**Alt** + **=**
B) Select **O** (Font)		**O**

5. Select **S** (Size) . . . . **S**

6. Select **one** of the following: Option

   a) **P** (Superscript) . . . . **P**

   b) **B** (Subscript) . . . . **B**

   c) **F** (Fine) . . . . **F**

   d) **S** (Small) . . . . **S**

   e) **L** (Large) . . . . **L**

   f) **V** (Very Large) . . . . **V**

   g) **E** (Extra Large) . . . . **E**

NOTE: *Sizes are relative to the base font, and depend on what fonts are available for printer. If a size is unavailable, the closest available size will be substituted.*

186

Fonts (continued)

CHANGING APPEARANCE OF FONT

BEFORE TYPING TEXT

1. Place cursor on line where font appearance change will begin.

2. Press **Ctrl + F8** (Font) . . . . **Ctrl** + **F8**

OR	Pull-down Menu	OR
A) Press **Alt + =**		**Alt** + **=**
B) Select **O** (Font)		**O**

3. Select **A** (Appearance) . . . . **A**

4. Select **one** of the following: **Option**

    a) **B** (Bold) . . . . **B**

    b) **U** (Underline) . . . . **U**

    c) **D** (Double Underline) . . . . **D**

    d) **I** (Italic) . . . . **I**

    e) **O** (Outline) . . . . **O**

    f) **A** (Shadow) . . . . **A**

    g) **C** (Small **C**aps) . . . . **C**

    h) **R** (Redline) . . . . **R**

    i) **S** (Strikeout) . . . . **S**

> *NOTE: Appearances are relative to the base font, and depend on what fonts are available for printer. If an appearance is unavailable, the closest available appearance will be substituted.*

5. Type text.

6. Press **Right Arrow** (restore original setting) . .

Fonts (continued)
Changing Appearance of Font (continued)

EXISTING TEXT

1. Place cursor on first character of text to be changed.

2. Press **Alt + F4** (Block) . . . . `Alt`+`F4`

OR	Pull-down Menu	OR
A) Press **Alt + =**		`Alt`+`=`
B) Select **E** (Edit)		`E`
C) Select **B** (Block)		`B`

3. Highlight text (See Block Text on page 10).

4. Press **Ctrl + F8** (Font) . . . . `Ctrl`+`F8`

OR	Pull-down Menu	OR
A) Press **Alt + =**		`Alt`+`=`
B) Select **O** (Font)		`O`

5. Select **A** (Appearance) . . . . `A`

Continued ...

188

6. Select **one** of the following: **Option**

  a) **B** (Bold) . . . .   **B**

  b) **U** (Underline) . . . .   **U**

  c) **D** (Double Underline) . . . .   **D**

  e) **I** (Italic) . . . .   **I**

  f) **O** (Outline) . . . .   **O**

  g) **A** (Shadow) . . . .   **A**

  h) **C** (Small **C**aps) . . . .   **C**

  i) **R** (Redline) . . . .   **R**

  j) **S** (Strikeout) . . . .   **S**

*NOTE: Appearances are relative to the base
font, and depend on what fonts are
available for printer. If an appearance
is unavailable, the closest available
appearance will be substituted.*

PRINT COLOR

CHANGING PRINT COLOR

1. Place cursor on line where print color change
   will begin.

2. Press **Ctrl + F8** (Font) . . . .   **Ctrl** + **F8**

OR	**Pull-down Menu**	OR
A) Press **Alt + =**		**Alt** + **=**
B) Select **O** (Font)		**O**

3. Select **C** (Print Color) . . . .   **C**

Continued ...

Fonts (continued)
Print Color (continued)
Changing Print Color (continued)

4. Select **one** of the following: Option

   a) **K** (Black) . . . .   `K`

   b) **W** (White) . . . .   `W`

   c) **R** (Red) . . . .   `R`

   d) **G** (Green) . . . .   `G`

   e) **B** (Blue) . . . .   `B`

   f) **Y** (Yellow) . . . .   `Y`

   g) **M** (Magenta) . . . .   `M`

   h) **C** (Cyan) . . . .   `C`

   i) **E** (Orange) . . . .   `E`

   j) **A** (Gray) . . . .   `A`

   k) **N** (Brown) . . . .   `N`

5. Press **F7** (return to document) . . . .   `F7`

6. Type text.

7. Press **Ctrl + F8** (Font) . . . .   `Ctrl`+`F8`

OR	Pull-down Menu	OR
A) Press **Alt + =**		`Alt`+`=`
B) Select **O** (Font)		`O`

8. Select **C** (Print Color) . . . .   `C`

9. Select **K** (Black) . . . .   `K`

10. Press **F7** (return to document) . . . .   `F7`

Fonts (continued)

CREATING A PRINT COLOR

1. Place cursor on line where print color change will begin.

2. Press **Ctrl + F8** (Font) . . . . `Ctrl`+`F8`

OR	Pull-down Menu	OR
A) Press **Alt + =**	`Alt`+`=`	
B) Select **O** (Font)		`O`

3. Select **C** (Print Color) . . . . `C`

4. Select **O** (Other) . . . . `O`

5. Type percentage of red . . . . Number

6. **Enter** . . . . `⏎`

7. Type percentage of green . . . . Number

8. **Enter** . . . . `⏎`

9. Type percentage of blue . . . . Number

10. **Enter** . . . . `⏎`

11. Press **F7** (return to document) . . . . `F7`

12. Type text.

13. Press **Ctrl + F8** (Font) . . . . `Ctrl`+`F8`

OR	Pull-down Menu	OR
A) Press **Alt + =**	`Alt`+`=`	
B) Select **O** (Font)		`O`

14. Select **C** (Print Color) . . . . `C`

15. Select **K** (Black) . . . . `K`

16. Press **F7** (return to document) . . . . `F7`

GRAPHICS

CREATE GRAPHIC BOX

1. Press Alt + F9 (Graphics) .... `Alt`+`F9`

OR	Pull-down Menu	OR
A) Press **Alt + =**		`Alt`+`=`
B) Select **G** (Graphics)		`G`
---

2. Select **one** of the following: Option

    a) **F** (Figure) .... `F`

    b) **T** (Table) .... `T`

    c) **B** (Text Box) .... `B`

    d) **U** (User Box) .... `U`

    e) **E** (Equation) .... `E`

3. Select **C** (Create) .... `C`

4. Define Graphic Box (see Define Graphic Box).

   Graphic Definitions include: Filename, Contents, Caption, Anchor Type, Vertical Position, Horizontal Position, Size, Wrap Text Around Box and Edit.

5. Press **F7** (return to document) .... `F7`

EDIT GRAPHIC BOX

1. Press **Alt + F9** (Graphics) . . . . `Alt`+`F9`

OR	Pull-down Menu	OR
A) Press **Alt + =**		`Alt`+`=`
B) Select **G** (Graphics)		`G`

2. Select **one** of the following: **Option**

   a) **F** (Figure) . . . . `F`

   b) **T** (Table) . . . . `T`

   c) **B** (Text Box) . . . . `B`

   d) **U** (User Box) . . . . `U`

   e) **E** (Equation) . . . . `E`

3. Select **E** (Edit) . . . . `E`

4. Type number of existing graphic . . . . Number

5. Define Graphic Box (see Define Graphic Box).

   Graphic Definitions include: Filename, Contents, Caption, Anchor Type, Vertical Position, Horizontal Position, Size, Wrap Text Around Box and Edit.

6. **Enter** . . . . `↵`

7. Press **F7** (return to document) . . . . `F7`

Graphics (continued)

NEW NUMBER

1. Place cursor before graphic box (see Reveal Codes).

2. Press **Alt + F9** (Graphics) .... **Alt**+**F9**

OR	Pull-down Menu	OR
A) Press **Alt + =**		**Alt**+**=**
B) Select **G** (Graphics)		**G**

3. Select **one** of the following: **Option**

   a) **F** (Figure) .... **F**

   b) **T** (Table) .... **T**

   c) **B** (Text Box) .... **B**

   d) **U** (User Box) .... **U**

   e) **E** (Equation) .... **E**

4. Select **N** (New Number) .... **N**

5. Type new graphic number .... Number

6. Press **F7** (return to document) **F7**

CHANGE BORDER STYLE

1. Press **Alt + F3** (Reveal Codes) ...... **Alt**+**F3**

OR	Pull-down Menu	OR
A) Press **Alt + =**		**Alt**+**=**
B) Select **E** (Edit)		**E**
C) Select **R** (Reveal Codes)		**R**

Continued ...

194

Graphics (continued)
Border Style (continued)

2. Place cursor before graphic code to be changed.

3. Press **Alt + F3** (Reveal Codes) ...... `Alt`+`F3`

OR	Pull-down Menu	OR
A) Press **Alt + =**		`Alt`+`=`
B) Select **E** (Edit)		`E`
C) Select **R** (Reveal Codes)		`R`

4. Press **Alt + F9** (Graphics) .... `Alt`+`F9`

OR	Pull-down Menu	OR
A) Press **Alt + =**		`Alt`+`=`
B) Select **G** (Graphics)		`G`

5. Select **one** of the following: **Option**

   a) **F** (Figure) .... `F`

   b) **T** (Table) .... `T`

   c) **B** (Text Box) .... `B`

   d) **U** (User Box) .... `U`

   e) **E** (Equation) .... `E`

6. Select **O** (Options) .... `O`

Continued ...

Graphics (continued)
Border Style (continued)

7. Select **B** (Border Style) . . . . ☐B

8. Select **one** of the following **for each:**   Option
   (Left, Right, Top and Bottom sides of box)

   a) **N** (None) . . . . ☐N

   b) **S** (Single) . . . . ☐S

   c) **D** (Double) . . . . ☐D

   d) **A** (Dashed) . . . . ☐A

   e) **O** (Dotted) . . . . ☐O

   f) **T** (Thick) . . . . ☐T

   g) **E** (Extra Thick) . . . . ☐E

9. Press **F7** (return to document) . . . . ☐F7

GRAY SHADING

1. Press **Alt + F3** (Reveal Codes) . . . . . . ☐Alt + ☐F3

OR	Pull-down Menu	OR
A) Press **Alt + =**		☐Alt + ☐=
B) Select **E** (Edit)		☐E
C) Select **R** (Reveal Codes)		☐R

2. Place cursor before graphic code to be shaded.

Continued ...

196

Graphics (continued)
Gray Shading (continued)

3. Press **Alt + F3** (Reveal Codes) ...... `Alt`+`F3`

OR	Pull-down Menu	OR
A) Press **Alt + =**		`Alt`+`=`
B) Select **E** (Edit)		`E`
C) Select **R** (Reveal Codes)		`R`

4. Press **Alt + F9** (Graphics) .... `Alt`+`F9`

5. Select **one** of the following: **Option**

   a) **F** (Figure) .... `F`

   b) **T** (Table) .... `T`

   c) **B** (Text Box) .... `B`

   d) **U** (User Box) .... `U`

   e) **E** (Equation) .... `E`

6. Select **O** (Options) .... `O`

7. Select **G** (Gray Shading - % of black) .... `G`

8. Type percentage .... Number

9. **Enter** .... `⏎`

10. Press **F7** (return to document) .... `F7`

Graphics (continued)

CREATE HORIZONTAL LINE

1. Press **Alt + F9** (Graphics) . . . . `Alt`+`F9`

OR	Pull-down Menu	OR
A) Press **Alt + =**		`Alt`+`=`
B) Select **G** (Graphics)		`G`

2. Select **L** (Line) . . . . `L`

3. Select **H** (Horizontal Line) . . . . `H`

4. Select **one or more** of the following: Option

  a) **H** (Horizontal Position) . . . . `H`

    Select **one** of the following: Option

     1) **L** (Left) . . . . `L`

     2) **R** (Right) . . . . `R`

     3) **C** (Center) . . . . `C`

     4) **F** (Full) . . . . `F`

     5) **S** (Set Position:) . . . . `S`

       a. Type position . . . . Number

       b. **Enter** . . . . `↵`

Continued ...

Graphics (continued)
Create Horizontal Line (continued)

	Option
b) V (Vertical Position)	**V**

Select **one** of the following: **Option**

	Option
1) B (Baseline)	**B**
2) S (Set Position:)	**S**
a. Type position	Number
b. Enter	**↵**
c) L (Length of Line)	**L**
1) Type length	Number
2) Enter	**↵**
d) W (Width of Line)	**W**
1) Type width	Number
2) Enter	**↵**
e) G (Gray Shading - % of black)	**G**
1) Type percent	Number
2) Enter	**↵**
5. Press **F7** (return to document)	**F7**

Graphics (continued)

EDIT HORIZONTAL LINE

1. Press **Alt + F3** (Reveal Codes) . . . . `Alt`+`F3`

OR	Pull-down Menu	OR
A) Press **Alt + =**		`Alt`+`=`
B) Select **E** (Edit)		`E`
C) Select **R** (Reveal Codes)		`R`

2. Place cursor after Horizontal line code to be changed.

3. Press **Alt + F9** (Graphics) . . . . `Alt`+`F9`

OR	Pull-down Menu	OR
A) Press **Alt + =**		`Alt`+`=`
B) Select **G** (Graphics)		`G`

4. Select **L** (Line) . . . . `L`

5. Select **O** (Horizontal) . . . . `O`

6. Select **one or more** of the following: **Option**

  a) **H** (Horizontal Position) . . . . `H`

    Select **one** of the following: **Option**

    1) **L** (Left) . . . . `L`

    2) **R** (Right) . . . . `R`

    3) **C** (Center) . . . . `C`

    4) **F** (Full) . . . . `F`

    5) **S** (Set Position:) . . . . `S`

      a. Type position . . . . Number

      b. **Enter** . . . . `↵`

Continued ...

200

	Option
b) **V** (Vertical Position)	**V**

Select **one** of the following: **Option**

1) **B** (Baseline)	**B**
2) **S** (Set Position:)	**S**
a. Type position	Number
b. **Enter**	⏎
c) **L** (Length of Line)	**L**
1) Type length	Number
2) **Enter**	⏎
d) **W** (Width of Line)	**W**
Type width	Number
e) **G** (Gray Shading - % of black)	**G**
1) Type percent	Number
2) **Enter**	⏎
7. Press **F7** (return to document)	**F7**
8. Press **Alt** + **F3** (Reveal Codes)	**Alt**+**F3**

OR	Pull-down Menu	OR
A) Press **Alt** + **=**		**Alt**+**=**
B) Select **E** (Edit)		**E**
C) Select **R** (Reveal Codes)		**R**

CREATE VERTICAL LINE

1. Press **Alt + F9** (Graphics) . . . . `Alt`+`F9`

OR	Pull-down Menu	OR
A) Press **Alt + =**		`Alt`+`=`
B) Select **G** (Graphics)		`G`

2. Select **L** (Line) . . . . `L`

3. Select **V** (Vertical Line) . . . . `V`

4. Select **one or more** of the following: Option

  a) **H** (Horizontal Position) . . . . `H`

    Select **one** of the following: Option

    1) **L** (Left) . . . . `L`

    2) **R** (Right) . . . . `R`

    3) **B** (Between Columns) . . . . `B`

    4) **S** (Set Position:) . . . . `S`

      a. Type position . . . . Number

      b. Enter . . . . `↵`

Continued ...

Graphics (continued)
Create Vertical Line (continued)

	Option
b) **V** (Vertical Position)	**V**

Select **one** of the following: **Option**

1) **F** (Full Page)	**F**
2) **T** (Top)	**T**
3) **C** (Center)	**C**
4) **B** (Bottom)	**B**
2) **S** (Set Position:)	**S**
a. Type position	Number
b. **Enter**	⏎
c) **L** (Length of Line)	**L**
1) Type length	Number
2) **Enter**	⏎
d) **W** (Width of Line)	**W**
1) Type width	Number
2) **Enter**	⏎
e) **G** (Gray Shading - % of black)	**G**
1) Type percent	Number
2) **Enter**	⏎
5. Press **F7** (return to document)	**F7**

EDIT VERTICAL LINE

1. Press **Alt + F3** (Reveal Codes) ...... `Alt`+`F3`

OR	Pull-down Menu	OR
A) Press **Alt + =**		`Alt`+`=`
B) Select **E** (Edit)		`E`
C) Select **R** (Reveal Codes)		`R`

2. Place cursor after Vertical line code to be changed.

3. Press **Alt + F9** (Graphics) .... `Alt`+`F9`

OR	Pull-down Menu	OR
A) Press **Alt + =**		`Alt`+`=`
B) Select **G** (Graphics)		`G`

4. Select **L** (Line) .... `L`

5. Select **E** (Vertical) .... `E`

6. Select **one or more** of the following: Option

  a) **H** (Horizontal Position) .... `H`

    Select **one** of the following: Option

    1) **L** (Left) .... `L`

    2) **R** (Right) .... `R`

    3) **B** (Between Columns) .... `B`

    4) **S** (Set Position:) ...... `S`

      a. Type position .... Number

      b. **Enter** .... `↵`

Continued ...

Graphics (continued)
Edit Vertical Line (continued)

Option

b) **V** (Vertical Position) . . . . **V**

Select **one** of the following: Option

  1) **F** (Full Page) . . . . **F**

  2) **T** (Top) . . . . **T**

  3) **C** (Center) . . . . **C**

  4) **B** (Bottom) . . . . **B**

  2) **S** (Set Position:) . . . . **S**

    a. Type position . . . . Number

    b. **Enter** . . . . ⏎

c) **L** (Length of Line) . . . . **L**

  a) Type length . . . . Number

  b) **Enter** . . . . ⏎

d) **W** (Width of Line) . . . . **W**

  a) Type width . . . . Number

  b) **Enter** . . . . ⏎

e) **G** (Gray Shading - % of black) . . . . **G**

  a) Type percent . . . . Number

  b) **Enter** . . . . ⏎

7. Press **F7** (return to document) **F7**

Continued ...

Graphics (continued)
Edit Vertical Line (continued)

8. Press **Alt** + **F3** (Reveal Codes) ...... Alt + F3

OR	Pull-down Menu	OR
A) Press **Alt** + = ...		Alt + =
B) Select **E** (Edit)		E
C) Select **R** (Reveal Codes)		R

GRAPHIC DEFINITIONS

To access the Definition Screen, create or edit a graphic box (Figure, Table Box, Text Box, User Box, or Equation).

FILENAME

1. Create or Edit Graphic Box (see pages 191 and 192).

2. Select **F** (Filename) . . . . **F**

3. Type filename . . . . **Filename**

   NOTE: To retrieve text, type the name of a WordPerfect text file. To retrieve a graphic, type the name of a supported graphic file.

4. **Enter** . . . . ↵

5. **F7** (return to document) **F7**

CONTENTS

Determines which editor (i.e. Equation, Graphics, or Text) will be displayed when you select the Edit option:

1. Create or Edit Graphic Box (see pages 191 and 192).

2. Select **O** (Contents) . . . . **O**

3. Select **one** of the following: **Option**

   a) **G** (Graphic) . . . . **G**

   b) **D** (Graphic on **D**isk) . . . . **D**

   c) **T** (Text) . . . . **T**

   d) **E** (Equation) . . . . **E**

4. **F7** (return to document) **F7**

Graphics (continued)

CAPTION

1. Create or Edit Graphic Box (see pages 191 and 192).
2. Select **C** (Caption) .... `C`
3. Type or edit caption.
4. **Enter** .... `⏎`
5. **F7** (return to document) .... `F7`

ANCHOR TYPE

Determines how graphics box will be positioned with text.
1. Create or Edit Graphic Box (see pages 191 and 192).
2. Select **T** (Type) .... `T`
3. Select **one** of the following: **Option**

   a) **P** (Paragraph) .... `P`

   b) **A** (Page) .... `A`

   c) **C** (Character) .... `C`
4. **F7** (return to document) .... `F7`

Graphic Definitions (continued)

VERTICAL POSITION

Vertical Position is dependent on your Anchor Type selection

1. Create or Edit Graphic Box (see pages 191 and 192).

2. Select **V** (Vertical Position) . . . . **V**

   Character Anchor Type (relation to text baseline)

   Select **one** of the following: **Option**

   a) **T** (Top) . . . . **T**

   b) **C** (Center) . . . . **C**

   c) **B** (Bottom) . . . . **B**

   Page Anchor Type

   a) Type number of pages to skip . . . . . Number

   b) **Enter** . . . . **↵**

   c) Select **V** (Vertical Position) . . . . **V**

   d) Select **one** of the following: **Option**

   1) **F** (Full Page) . . . . **F**

   2) **T** (Top) . . . . **T**

   3) **C** (Center) . . . . **C**

   4) **B** (Bottom) . . . . **B**

   5) **S** (Set) . . . . **S**

      a. Type offset from top of page. Number

      b. **Enter** . . . . **↵**

Continued ...

Graphic Definitions (continued)
Vertical Position (continued)

Paragraph Anchor Type

a) Type offset from top of paragraph . .   Number

b) **Enter** .... ⏎

3. **F7** (return to document) F7

HORIZONTAL POSITION
Horizontal Position is dependent on your Anchor Type selection.
1. Create or Edit Graphic Box (see pages 191 and 192).

2. Select **H** (Horizontal Position) .... H

Character Anchor Type
Horizontal Position is not an option for this anchor type.
Page Anchor Type

Select **one** of the following: **Option**

a) **M** (Margins) .... M

Select **one** of the following: **Option**

1) **L** (Left) L

2) **R** (Right) .... R

3) **C** (Center) C

4) **F** (Full) .... F

Continued ...

Graphic Definitions (continued)
Horizontal Position (Page Anchor Type continued)

    Option

  b) **C** (Columns) .... **C**

    1) Type column number ...... Number

    2) **Enter** .... ↵

    3) Select **one** of the following: **Option**

      a. **L** (Left) .... **L**

      b. **R** (Right) .... **R**

      c. **C** (Center) .... **C**

      d. **F** (Full) .... **F**

  c) **S** (Set Position) .... **S**

    1) Type offset from left of page. Number

    2) **Enter** .... ↵

Paragraph Anchor Type

Select **one** of the following: **Option**

1) **L** (Left) .... **L**

2) **R** (Right) .... **R**

3) **C** (Center) .... **C**

4) **F** (Full) .... **F**

3. **F7** (return to document) **F7**

Graphic Definitions (continued)

SIZE

1. Create or Edit Graphic Box (see pages 191 and 192).

2. Select **S** (Size) .... S

3. Select **one** of the following: **Option**

   a) **W** (Set Width/Auto Height) .... W

      1) Type number (Width) .... Number

      2) **Enter** .... ⏎

   b) **H** (Set Height/Auto Width) .... H

      1) Type number (Height) .... Number

      2) **Enter** .... ⏎

   c) **B** (Set Both) .... B

      1) Type number (Width) .... Number

      2) **Enter** .... ⏎

      3) Type number (Height) .... Number

      4) **Enter** .... ⏎

   d) **A** (Auto Both) .... A

Graphic Definitions (continued)

WRAP TEXT AROUND BOX

1. Create or Edit Graphic Box (see pages 191 and 192).

2. Select **W** (Wrap Text Around Box) . . . . ⬛**W**

3. Type **Y** (Yes) . . . . ⬛**Y**

   OR   **OR**

   Type **N** (No) . . . . ⬛**N**

EDIT (Graphic Definition)

> *NOTE:* *The editor displayed will depend on the content of the graphic box. See Graphic Editor, Text Editor, Equation Editor.*

GRAPHIC EDITOR

> *NOTE:* *For use of this editor the Contents option must read or be changed to Graphic or Graphic on Disk. See Contents (Graphic Definitions) in this section.*

1. Create or Edit Graphic Box (see pages 191 and 192).

2. Select **E** (Edit) . . . . ⬛**E**

3. Select **one** of the following: **Option**

   a) **M** (Move) . . . . ⬛**M**

      1) Type horizontal movement . . . . . . Number

      2) **Enter** . . . . ⬛↵

      3) Type vertical movement . . . . Number

      4) **Enter** . . . . ⬛↵

   > *NOTE:* *Negative values move left and down respectively for horizontal and vertical.* ***Arrow keys*** *may also be used to move a graphic.* ***Ctrl-Home*** *resets changes.*

Continued ...

Graphic Definitions (continued)
Graphic Editor (continued)

                                                            Option

b) **S** (Scale) . . . . $\boxed{S}$

    1) Type x scale . . . . Number

    2) **Enter** . . . . $\boxed{\enter}$

    3) Type y scale . . . . Number

    4) **Enter** . . . . $\boxed{\enter}$

NOTE: *PgUp and PgDn may also be used to change scale of graphic.*

c) **R** (Rotate) . . . . $\boxed{R}$

    1) Type number of degrees . . . . Number

    2) **Enter** . . . . $\boxed{\enter}$

NOTE: *+ or - keys may also be used to rotate a graphic.*

d) **I**   (Invert on/off) . . . . $\boxed{I}$

e) **B** (Black & White) . . . . $\boxed{B}$

    Type **Y** (Yes) . . . . $\boxed{Y}$

    OR   **OR**

    Type **N** (No) . . . . $\boxed{N}$

4. Press **F7** (exit editor) . . . . $\boxed{F7}$

5. Press **F7** (return to document) . . . . $\boxed{F7}$

214

TEXT EDITOR

> *NOTE:* *For use of this editor the Contents option must read or be changed to Text or Empty. See Contents (Graphic Definitions) in this section.*

1. Create or Edit Graphic Box (see pages 191 and 192).

2. Select **E** (Edit) . . . . **E**

3. Type or edit text.

> *NOTE:* *Most of WordPerfect's editing features are available from this text box editor.*

ROTATE TEXT (Option)

   a) Press **Alt + F9** (Graphics) . . . .

   b) Select **one** of the following: **Option**

      1) **1** (0°) **1**

      2) **2** (90°) **2**

      3) **3** (180°) **3**

      4) **4** (270°) **4**

4. Press **F7** (exit editor) **F7**

5. Press **F7** (return to document) **F7**

EQUATION EDITOR

NOTE: For use of this editor the Contents option must read or be changed to Equation. See Contents (Graphic Definitions) in this section.

1. Create or Edit Graphic Box (see pages 191 and 192).

2. Select **E** (Edit) ....

CREATE OR EDIT EQUATION

Type equation.
Example: Type 3 times 4 over 5

NOTE: Use Backspace or Delete to remove typed characters.

BUILD EQUATION USING EQUATION PALETTE

a) Press **F5** to access palette window ......

b) Use cursor movement keys to highlight desired command or symbol.

NOTE: Press PgDn or PgUp to access additional screens of symbols.

c) **Enter** ....

VIEW EQUATION (DISPLAY WINDOW)

Press **Ctrl + F3** (Screen) ....

Continued ...

Graphic Definitions (continued)
Equation Editor (continued)

POSITION VIEW AND SCALE OF EQUATION

*NOTE: This feature affects only the view and
scale within the Display Window.*

a) Press **Shift + F3** (Switch) ...... `Shift`+`F3`

b) Use the following to change view/scale: **Option**

Arrow keys
(move within view) .. `←` `→` `↑` `↓`

PgUp (increase scale) .... `PgUp`

PgDn (decrease scale) .... `PgDn`

Ctrl + Home (reset scale) ... `Ctrl`+`Home`

c) Press **F7** (exit to editor) .... `F7`

SAVE EQUATION TO DISK

a) Press **F10** (Save) .... `F10`

b) Type equation filename .... **Filename**

c) **Enter** .... `↵`

PRINT EQUATION AS GRAPHIC OR TEXT MODE

a) Press **Shift + F1** (Setup) .... `Shift`+`F1`

b) Select **P** (Print as Graphics) .... `P`

c) Type **Y** (Yes) .... `Y`

OR   **OR**

Type **N** (No) .... `N`

d) Press **F7** (exit to equation editor) .... `F7`

*NOTE: To print equations in text mode,
WordPerfect will print symbols missing
from the font characters graphically.*

Continued ...

Graphic Definitions (continued)

GRAPHICAL FONT SIZE OF EQUATION

   a) Press **Shift + F1** (Setup) . . . . **Shift** + **F1**

   b) Select **G** (Graphical Font Size) . . . . **G**

   c) Select **D** (Default size) . . . . **D**

     OR   OR

     Select **S** (**S**et point size) . . . . **S**

        a) Type point size . . . . Number

        b) **Enter** . . . . ⏎

   d) Press **F7** (exit to equation editor) **F7**

3. Press **F7** (exit to document) **F7**

218
STYLES
CREATE

1. Press **Alt + F8** (Styles) . . . . `Alt`+`F8`

OR	Pull-down Menu	OR
1) Press **Alt + =**		`Alt`+`=`
2) Select **L** (Layout)		`L`
3) Select **S** (Styles)		`S`

2. Select **C** (Create) . . . . `C`

3. Select **N** (Name) . . . . `N`

4. Type name of style . . . . Style name

5. **Enter** . . . . `⏎`

6. Select **D** (Description) . . . . `D`

7. Type description of style.

8. **Enter** . . . . `⏎`

9. Select **T** (Type) . . . . `T`

10. Select **one** of the following: Option

   a) **P** (Paired) . . . . `P`

   b) **O** (Open) . . . . `O`

   c) **T** (Outline) . . . . `T`

11. Select **C** (Codes) . . . . `C`

12. Insert codes or text.

13. Press **F7** . . . . `F7`

Continued ...

219

Styles (continued)
Create (continued)

14. Select **E** (Enter) .... `E`

   NOTE: This selection is for paired styles only and
           *tells WordPerfect which function **Enter***
           should perform when the style is used.

15. Select **one** of the following: **Option**

   a) **H** (Hrt) .... `H`

   b) **F** (Off) .... `F`

   c) **O** (Off/On) .... `O`

16. Press **F7** .... `F7`

17. Press **F7** (return to document) .... `F7`

USING PAIRED STYLE FOR NEW TEXT

1. Place cursor where paired style will begin.

2. Press Alt + F8 (Style) .... `Alt`+`F8`

OR	Pull-down Menu	OR
A) Press **Alt + =**		`Alt`+`=`
B) Select **L** (Layout)		`L`
C) Select **S** (Styles)		`S`

3. Use cursor movement keys to highlight desired style.

4. Select **O** (On) .... `O`

5. Type text.

6. Press **Right Arrow** (turn style off) .... `→`

220

USING PAIRED STYLE FOR EXISTING TEXT

1. Place cursor where paired style will begin.

2. Press **Alt + F4** (Block) . . . . `Alt`+`F4`

OR	Pull-down Menu	OR
A) Press **Alt + =**		`Alt`+`=`
B) Select **E** (Edit)		`E`
C) Select **B** (Block)		`B`

3. Highlight text (see Block Text on page 10).

4. Press **Alt + F8** (Style) . . . . `Alt`+`F8`

OR	Pull-down Menu	OR
A) Press **Alt + =**		`Alt`+`=`
B) Select **L** (Layout)		`L`
C) Select **S** (Styles)		`S`

5. Use cursor movement keys to highlight desired style.

6. Select **O** (On) . . . . `O`

Styles (continued)

USING OPEN STYLE

1. Place cursor where style will be inserted.

2. Press **Alt** + **F8** (Style) . . . .

OR	Pull-down Menu	OR
A) Press **Alt** + = ...		
B) Select **L** (Layout)		
C) Select **S** (Styles)		

3. Use cursor movement keys to highlight desired style.

4. Select **O** (On) . . . .

EDIT STYLES

1. Press **Alt** + **F8** (Style) . . . .

OR	Pull-down Menu	OR
A) Press **Alt** + = ...		
B) Select **L** (Layout)		
C) Select **S** (Styles)		

2. Use cursor movement keys to highlight desired style.

3. Select **E** (Edit) . . . .

4. Edit Style options.

   NOTE: Style Edit options include the Name, Type, Description, Codes and use of Enter for the highlighted style. See Create Style in this section.

5. **Enter** . . . .

6. Press **F7** (return to document) . . . .

222

Styles (continued)

DELETE STYLES

1. Press **Alt + F8** (Style) . . . . ⎇Alt + F8

OR	Pull-down Menu	OR
A) Press **Alt + =**		⎇Alt + ▣
B) Select **L** (Layout)		Ⓛ
C) Select **S** (Styles)		Ⓢ

2. Use cursor movement keys to highlight desired style.

3. Select **D** (Delete) . . . . Ⓓ

4. Select **one** of the following: **Option**

    a) **L** (Leaving Codes) . . . . Ⓛ

    b) **I** (Including Codes) . . . . Ⓘ

    c) **D** (Definition Only) . . . . Ⓓ

5. Press **F7** (return to document) F7

SAVE/UPDATE STYLES LIST

1. Press **Alt + F8** (Style) . . . . ⎇Alt + F8

OR	Pull-down Menu	OR
A) Press **Alt + =**		⎇Alt + ▣
B) Select **L** (Layout)		Ⓛ
C) Select **S** (Styles)		Ⓢ

2. Select **S** (Save) . . . . Ⓢ

3. Type name of style list.

4. **Enter** . . . . ↵

    NOTE: Type Y to update style document if it already exists.

5. Press **F7** (return to document) F7

Styles (continued)

RETRIEVE STYLES LIST

1. Press **Alt + F8** (Style) . . . . `Alt`+`F8`

OR	Pull-down Menu	OR
A) Press **Alt + =**		`Alt`+`=`
B) Select **L** (Layout)		`L`
C) Select **S** (Styles)		`S`

2. Select **R** (Retrieve) . . . . `R`

3. Type name of style list.

4. **Enter** . . . . `↵`

5. Press **F7** (return to document) . . . . `F7`

PASSWORD

ADD/CHANGE

1. Retrieve document that will be password protected.

2. Press **Ctrl + F5** (Text In/Out) . . . . `Ctrl`+`F5`

3. Select **P** (Password) . . . . `P`

OR	Pull-down Menu	OR
A) Press **Alt + =**		`Alt`+`=`
B) Select **F** (File)		`F`
C) Select **W** (Password)		`W`

4. Select **A** (Add/Change) . . . . `A`

5. Type password (up to 24 characters)

6. **Enter** . . . . `↵`

Continued ...

224

Password (continued)
Add/Change (continued)

7. Type password again.

8. **Enter** .... ⏎

REMOVE

1. Retrieve document that contains password to be removed.

2. Press **Ctrl + F5** (Text In/Out) .... `Ctrl`+`F5`

3. Select **P** (Password) .... `P`

4. Select **R** (Remove) .... `R`

ADVANCE

Signals printer to advance to a specific position in documer
1. Place cursor where advance will begin.

2. Press **Shift + F8** (Format) .... `Shift`+`F8`

OR	Pull-down Menu	OR
A) Press **Alt + =**		`Alt`+`=`
B) Select **L** (Layout)		`L`

3. Select **O** (Other) .... `O`

4. Select **A** (Advance) .... `A`

Continued ...

Advance (continued)

5. Select **one** of the following: **Option**

   a) **U** (Up) . . . . **U**

   b) **D** (Down) . . . . **D**

   c) **I** (LIne) . . . . **I**

   d) **L** (Left) . . . . **L**

   e) **R** (Right) . . . . **R**

   f) **P** (Position) . . . . **P**

6. Type advance number . . . . Number

7. **Enter** . . . . **⏎**

8. Press **F7** (return to document) **F7**

LINE NUMBERING

1. Retrieve document that will contain line numbering.

2. Press **Shift + F8** (Format) . . . . **Shift** + **F8**

OR	Pull-down Menu	OR
A) Press **Alt + =** . . . . **Alt** + **=**		
B) Select **L** (Layout) . . . . **L**		

3. Select **L** (Line Format) . . . . **L**

4. Select **N** (Line Numbering) . . . . **N**

5. Type **Y** . . . . **Y**

6. Press **F7** (return to document) **F7**

226
CHANGE WORD SPACING

1. Place cursor on line where change is to begin.

2. Press **Shift + F8** (Format) . . . . `Shift`+`F8`

OR	Pull-down Menu	OR

A) Press **Alt + =** . . . . `Alt`+`=`

B) Select **L** (Layout) . . . . `L`

3. Select **O** (Other) . . . . `O`

4. Select **P** (Printer Functions) . . . . `P`

5. Select **W** (Word Spacing) . . . . `W`

6. Select **one** of the following: Option

  a) **N** (Normal) . . . . `N`

  b) **O** (Optimal) . . . . `O`

  c) **P** (Percent of Optimal) . . . . `P`

  d) **S** (Set Pitch) . . . . `S`

7. Select **one** of the following: Option

  a) **N** (Normal) . . . . `N`

  b) **O** (Optimal) . . . . `O`

  c) **P** (Percent of Optimal) . . . . `P`

    1) Type percent of Optimal . . . . Number

    2) **Enter** . . . . `↵`

  d) **S** (Set Pitch) . . . . `S`

    1) Type pitch . . . . Number

    2) **Enter** . . . . `↵`

8. Press **F7** (return to document) . . . . `F7`

LINE HEIGHT

1. Place cursor on line where line height change is to begin.

2. Press **Shift + F8** (Format) . . . . `Shift`+`F8`

OR	Pull-down Menu	OR
A) Press **Alt + =**		`Alt`+`=`
B) Select **L** (Layout)		`L`

3. Select **L** (Line) . . . . `L`

4. Select **H** (Height) . . . . `H`

5. Select **A** (Auto) . . . . `A`

    OR   OR

    Select **F** (Fixed) . . . . `F`

        a) Type height . . . . Number

        b) **Enter** . . . . `↵`

7. Press **F7** (return to document) . . . . `F7`

KERNING ON/OFF

1. Place cursor before characters to be affected by setting.

2. Press **Shift + F8** (Format) . . . . `Shift`+`F8`

3. Select **O** (Other) . . . . `O`

4. Select **P** (Printer Functions) . . . . `P`

5. Select **K** (Kerning) . . . . `K`

6. Type **Y** (Yes) . . . . `Y`

    OR   OR

    Type **N** (No) . . . . `N`

7. Press **F7** . . . . `F7`

228

PRINTER COMMAND

Printer Commands send escape codes directly to printer.

1. Place cursor at desired position for printer command.

2. Press **Shift + F8** (Format) . . . . **Shift + F8**

OR	Pull-down Menu	OR
A) Press **Alt + =**		**Alt + =**
B) Select **L** (Layout)		**L**

3. Select **O** (Other) . . . . **O**

4. Select **P** (Printer Functions) . . . . **P**

5. Select **P** (Printer Command) . . . . **P**

6. Select **C** (Command) . . . . **C**

7. Type command.

8. **Enter** . . . . ⏎

9. Press **F7** (return to document) **F7**

SETUP

1. Press **Shift + F1** . . . . **Shift + F1**

OR	Pull-down Menu	OR
A) Press **Alt + =**		**Alt + =**
B) Select **F** (File)		**F**
C) Select **T** (Setup)		**T**

2. Make setup changes.

3. Press **F7** (return to document) **F7**

HELP

1. Press **F3** (Help) .... `F3`

OR	Pull-down Menu	OR
A) Press **Alt + =**		`Alt`+`=`
B) Select **H** (Help)		`H`
C) Select **H** (Help)		`H`

2. Look up feature.

3. **Enter** (to return to document) .... `⏎`

EXIT/QUIT

Note This does not save a document.
1. Press **F7** .... `F7`

OR	Pull-down Menu	OR
A) Press **Alt + =**		`Alt`+`=`
B) Select **F** (File)		`F`
C) Select **X** (Exit)		`X`

2. Type **N** .... `N`

3. Type **Y** .... `Y`

230

232

234